PROPHECY ON THE RIVER

RELATED PUBLICATIONS
FROM ATTAR BOOKS

People of the Earth
Peter Calvert, Richard Bentley
Carolyn Longden, Trisha Wren

The Lantern in the Skull
Hugh Major

The Luminous Nun
Kerryn Levy

The New Mysticism
Keith Hill

Prophecy on the River

Judith Hoch

attar books

First edition published in 2019 by Attar Books
Auckland, New Zealand.

Casebook ISBN 978-0-9951203-3-4
Paperback ISBN 978-0-9951203-4-1
Ebook ISBN 978-0-9951203-5-8

Copyright © Judith Hoch 2019
Introduction © Keith Hill 2019

The right of Judith Hoch to be identified as the author of this work in terms of Section 96 of the Copyright Act 1996 is hereby asserted.

All rights reserved. Copying and distributing passages excerpted from this book for the purpose of sharing and debating is permitted on the condition that (1) excerpts are brief, (2) the source of each excerpt is fully acknowledged, and (3) such excerpts are not onsold. Otherwise, except for fair dealing or brief passages quoted in a newspaper, magazine, radio, television or internet review, no part of this book may be reproduced in any form or by any means, or in any form of binding or cover other than that in which it is published, without permission in writing from the Publisher. This same condition is imposed on any subsequent purchaser.

Cover image: Shutterstock

Judith Hoch's website:
www.judithhoch.com

Attar Books is a New Zealand publisher that focuses on work which explores today's spiritual and mystical experiences, culture, concepts and practices. For more information on our publications visit the website:

www.attarbooks.com

Photo: Murray Hedwig

JUDITH HOCH'S eyes were first opened to the world of spirit, music, and Africa's rich oral traditions while carrying out doctoral research in western Nigeria, where she lived for two years among the Yoruba people. Her undergraduate work had been at Tulane in New Orleans, where she first encountered Vodou, while her Masters degree research was among Cree people in northcentral Quebec. This research made her very aware of the negative impacts of white colonialism.

After receiving her Ph.D. from McGill University, Judith held faculty posts at two Florida Universities, where she taught anthropology and oversaw student research. She later became an exhibiting artist. During this period, she exhibited widely, won a national competition, and gave numerous workshops to discuss her ideas and work, using her art to explore the depths of non-western spirituality and expose the holocaust of the European witch trials.

While living in Miami, Judith met a Yoruba priest, Ernesto Pichardo. He challenged her cultural assumptions around whiteness, and introduced her to Yoruba spiritual practices, including to her personal head Orisha, Elegguá/Eshu, the trickster. Judith also studied with the senior teachers of B.K.S Iyengar for many years, teaching at a yoga institute in Miami, and near her home in Aoteaora.

Judith and her husband John first arrived in New Zealand in the 1980s, where they bought land, built a house, and planted native trees. There she was strongly drawn to Māori, and especially to Aroha Ropata, whose warmth, generosity and love of Bob Marley made her seem like an islander from the Caribbean, and very Miamian.

Prophecy on the River has come out of this rich mix of travel, research, welcomed influences, and personal exploration.

CONTENTS

Reflections on "the Other"   9

PROPHECY ON THE RIVER

	Prologue	17
1	Veriditas	19
2	Waitaha Ancestors	28
3	Conversations with the Chief	38
4	I Am the Mountain	48
5	Taniwha Rising	56
6	The Pattern in the Water	67
7	Alone With the Trees	74
8	The Oldest Tree on the Mountain	84
9	Spirits that Rule the River	94
10	The Curse of Waitaha	100
11	Recharging the Land	110

Glossary   123
Bibliography   128
Acknowledgements   129

REFLECTIONS ON "THE OTHER"

MODERN NEW ZEALAND exists as a result of multiple waves of human migration. Māori were the first to arrive here, in the thirteenth century. Abel Tasman "discovered" the two main islands in 1642, his fellow Dutch geographers naming them Nova Zeelandia. In 1769 James Cook claimed the islands for the British Crown and renamed them New Zealand. The country officially became a British colony in 1840, when British officials and Māori chiefs signed the Treaty of Waitangi.

This occurred as part of worldwide European colonisation. To over-simplify a very complex process, during the fifteenth century European traders, driven by the desire to extend their nation's reach, to make their names, and to make their fortunes, sought out and brought back exotic goods to Europe: silk from China, saltpetre (for making gunpowder) from India, spices from Indonesia, sugar from Africa and the Carribean, and whale and seal oil extracted from the world's oceans. At the same time, the alluring chimera of making a fortune from gold sent prospectors scurrying across the globe.

To ensure supply lines remained open, European nations established colonial outposts in Asia, Africa, the Americas and the Pacific. Brutality was widespread. Rubber barons in South America used violence to force indigenous tribespeople to extract valuable latex from the Amazon's rubber trees. This fed Europe's industries, and enabled a handful of entrepreneurs to make fortunes accrued through the deaths of tens of thousands of tribespeople.

During the nineteenth century, when the most significant waves of soldiers, traders, clergy and colonising workers were launched, Europeans constructed the concept of the Other, identifying non-Europeans in terms of difference: different skin colours, body types, social norms and religious beliefs. The colonised spoke different languages, wore different clothes, ate different food, and believed very different things. European feelings about them were complicated. They needed workers, so many customs practised by those they colonised were tolerated. A handful, such as Richard Burton and Lawrence of Arabia, even found the exoticism alluring, actively embracing it. But most thought those they encountered strange, indecipherable and, in an irony lost on the self-entitled invaders, ungrateful. This made colonised peoples dangerous, which in turn generated fear.

To keep the potentially dangerous Other in its place, Europeans concocted polarities they used to separate themselves from those they encountered: white vs black (or yellow or brown), Christian vs heathen, rational vs irrational, sophisticated vs savage, master vs slave. For the colonisers, these descriptors enabled them to maintain their sense of superiority. For the colonised, the polarities formed chains that locked them into inferior social, economic, political and cultural status.

Following World War Two, most of the world's colonies began the process of transforming into self-governing states. New Zealand was granted independence from Britain in 1931. This was ratified by the New Zealand Parliament in 1947. In 1987, the Treaty of Waitangi was officially recognised as providing the legal basis of a bicultural partnership between Māori and Pākehā (white New Zealanders). At the same time, Māori was recognised as the country's co-official language, alongside English. However, the impacts of colonialisation, and the injustices and hurts that accompany being declared Other, were too deep-seated to be kissed better by Parliamentary decree. Healing remains a work-in-progress.

One of the great virtues of Judith Hoch's *Prophecy on the River* is the way she explores the echoing hurts, and offers a spiritual perspective on how deep healing may proceed. In this sense, the prophecy referred to in the title doesn't involve a foretelling of what will happen in the future. Nor is it a judgement on our national inadequacies: no Cassandra curse is made. Instead, Hoch's prophecy is a call to action. At its heart is a reminder that healing doesn't just involve us as human beings attempting to live peaceably together on the islands of Aotearoa. It involves the land that constitutes these islands, it involves the plants and creatures that today are struggling to live with us on it, and it involves the spiritual dimension that weaves through the land, through its ecosystems, and through each individual life.

Judith Hoch skilfully explores the cultural and historical background behind her call to action. In doing so, she reveals the extent to which the dichotomies that underpinned colonial assumptions regarding Māori inadequately reflect the complexity of what Otherness actually involves on the ground, in the forest, on the shoreline, across the land. By implication, the book shows that the colonial notion of the Other itself obscures rather than elucidates life "on the ground".

Judith Hoch's personal history underscores this. A migrant from the United States, when Judith arrived in Aotearoa the white European culture she encountered was decidedly Other compared to the multicultural milieu she had long been immersed in in Miami. Yet from Aotearoa's perspective, as a foreigner she herself was Other. However, her move to New Zealand was actually commonplace: in 2019 over a quarter of Aotearoa's population was born elsewhere.

This means that each of us—while using public transport, shopping in malls and supermarkets, or just crossing the street—daily come face-to-face with the Other in its many biological and cultural transformations. Conversely, it means we who are already here are Other for those who have recently arrived. The fear this situation stimulates in many is palpable, as witnessed by the Christchurch mosque shootings, which took place just a few days before I wrote this. But, equally, the awareness is growing that any sense of difference is subsumed into the consciousness that in reality we are all part of the one humanity.

This movement, too, is reflected in Judith's story. After more than three decades of residence here, during which she and her husband bought land, built a house on it, and reforested it with native plants, she has embraced biculturalism so well that she is more in tune with Aotearoa's Māori heritage than many Pākehā born here.

But appreciating that the fear of difference is rooted in colonial bias cannot end this discussion. Because the Other exists on another level again, beyond the geographical, the biological, the cultural. This Other is the domain of spirit. It is the domain of dreams and visions. It is an insubstantial arena where people have enigmatic and ecstatic encounters. In some instances, as with this book, it is the realm from which prophecies emanate. It is characterised as Other because it apparently exists in contrast to the physical world, and because for many this perceived difference engenders feelings of uncertainty and fear.

European rationalism decreed the spiritual and ancestral Other doesn't exist. Christian dogma maintained that engagement with it was heretical. In Europe, those who practised traditional mediumship and healing arts were among those accused of being witches and sorcerers, and were systematically hunted, arrested, tried, imprisoned and killed. As a result, during the period of European colonial expansion, the spiritual Other, embraced by indigenous peoples worldwide, was banned. The only permitted spiritual encounters took place in the sanctum of Christian churches and through the intercession of Christian priests. European colonialists brought this attitude to Aotearoa. For Māori, the 1907 Tohunga Suppression Act meant their tohunga (priests, healers and seers) were forced underground. Many ceased practising altogether. Yet the realm of the Other is where the ancestors reside. In *Prophecy on the River*, Judith offers a fascinating account of her interactions with the ancestors.

Interestingly, Judith's first encounter with Māoridom, which occurred within hours of arriving in Aotearoa, was on this spiritual level. It involved walking into an immovable sheet of transparent light on a path beside an urupā (Māori burial ground), which prevented her and her husband from moving forwards. Much later, she discovered that the wall of light may have been generated by a chief whose people died in 1886, during the devastating eruption of Mount Tarawera. But even this appreciation of the Other as involving ancestors is not as straightforward as this simple description implies.

Before arriving in New Zealand, Judith had honed her spiritual awareness through meditation and had learned to balance her energy through yoga. These practices helped her become sensitive to subtle spiritual impressions. In Miami, during her late twenties, she also met Ernesto Pichardo, a priest of the West African Yoruba god, Shango. Healer, medium and wisdom teacher, Ernesto became Judith's guide into the operations and intents of the spiritual realm.

Postmodern constructionists argue that the varieties of mystical encounters are created through culturally imposed suggestion: people are told that if they believe this, and practice that, such-and-such will occur. Ernesto's contribution to Judith's story contradicts this viewpoint. It is he, using skills developed within the West African and Cuban diaspora, who connected Judith with the deceased mother of her close friend, Aroha. Together, she and Aroha performed a ceremony to heal the wounded land, following ancestral instructions. Culturally, the activity occurred as a result of amalgamating North American, Māori and Afro/Cuban shamanic sensibilities. It led Judith to reach a level of understanding that transcended the particularities of each.

The intention behind this series is to explore the different ways New Zealanders mystically experience the spiritual. On the surface, *Prophecy on the River* is about the environment, *our* environment, and the damage industrialisation of the landscape has caused. But beyond this several more subtle themes are touched on.

One is that spiritual identities function as nature spirits, nurturing flora and fauna and the ecosystems they occupy. In this respect, Judith's account provides an on-the-ground view of how we may adopt a widescreen, spiritually-based concern for the natural world and the flora and fauna that need functioning ecosystems to survive.

Another key theme is that of our ancestral core, a concept Ernesto Pichard introduces. We automatically think of ancestors as ancient, but this is not necessarily the case. Once they leave their bodies, our parents, uncles, grandparents and siblings enter the realm of the ancestors.

In due course, so will we. It is in this sense that *Prophecy on the River* suggests we are mistaken calling that realm the Other—because if all spiritual identities derive from the same Source, and if we will each take our own place among the ancestors, then the spiritual Other is not really Other at all; the Other is us. This could equally be extended to flora and fauna. Every species plays a specialised role in the home we call the Earth. They add to our world. Without them, we would not exist. They are us, too.

In stressed times, when so many among us do not recognise the spiritual in themselves, let alone in other people, cultures or outlooks, and particularly not in the flora and fauna that share the Earth with us, this is an insight on which our continued existence may very well turn out to depend.

—Keith Hill, series editor

PROPHECY ON THE RIVER

The aim is to balance the terror of being alive
with the wonder of being alive.

— Carlos Castaneda

PROLOGUE

I LIVE IN A CLOUD FOREST in New Zealand. This year there is a drought and nearby paddocks are as yellow as the hills in California. Smaller trees on the edge of the forest are wilted and some have died. Up in the forest, the ground is dried and cracked in places. However, before long, as summer advances, the rainforest and mountain will seduce clouds to join them. Then a mist will move through the forest, mingling with the leaves in its canopy. After a while, a slow drip, drip, drip will fall from the canopy onto the forest floor, wetting dense thickets of vines, shining palm fronds, tall tree trunks. These droplets will multiply into rain. The fresh water will soak the land and roots, run into gullies and creeks, and flow fast to the Wainui River, churning and white capped. The Wainui River is the site of the spirit prophecy described in this book.

Natural scientists use the phrase "cloud stripping" to describe how the forest and mountains draw rain into our water system. Sometimes it doesn't rain; sometimes there are mighty rainfalls. Some of the most astounding are vividly described in *Prophecy on the River*.

New Zealand's Māori name is Aotearoa,[1] the Long White Cloud. *Aotea* means cloud; *roa*, long. Lost in the clouds, the Aotearoa islands are the most southern of the Polynesian island chains. I live in the South Island, also called Te Waipounamu. *Wai* is water, *pounamu* is

---

[1] A glossary of Māori and African Lucumi words is included at the end of the book.

the sacred, healing greenstone found only on Te Waipounamu. On Te Waipounamu, I live in Wainui Bay. Wainui means lots of water: *wai*, water; *nui*, big, a lot. In Wainui, my husband and I have named our land *Waitaha*, inspired by my friend Aroha Ropata and her mother, Netta, descended from the Waitaha tribes, whose stories portray them as the peaceful water containers of creation, gardeners and artists holding the gifts of the universe. Because of these strongly poetic Māori names, I have an image of myself surrounded by rainforest on a cloud island, where water flows from the mountains to the river and sea over an Earth full of magical stones.

I am from Miami, Florida, an immigrant to New Zealand. When I began writing this book, I thought of *The Enigma of Arrival*, one of my favourite books by V.S. Naipaul. Naipaul was an immigrant to Britain, from a much warmer place, living in a rural county. Displaced like him, I was a stranger to the landscape and culture of Aotearoa. Only during my morning walks did I start slowly untangling the surrounding landscape's mysteries. As you read *Prophecy on the River*, imagine walking with me by the river through the forest to the falls.

The Waitaha people of Aotearoa may have preceded the Māori peoples, leaving traces of their culture in many place names and local stories. Aroha walked the Greenstone Track with Barry Brailsford, author of *The Song of Waitaha*. She also played a part in reigniting the vigour of the coast near our land, when she and others placed impressive carved stones, infused with healing energy, on power spots. They were healing land and shoreline altered by decades of farming, forestry and conquest by the British and by Māori iwi (tribes). If the *Prophecy on the River* is fulfilled, Aotearoa will once again be a great Pacific nation of monumental forests, unique birds and peaceful people.

1. VERIDITAS

*Look after the birds and the forest flourishes.
If the forest flourishes, the birds flourish.*

— Māori proverb

ONE NIGHT IN WAINUI, WHILE STROLLING with my husband along the river bank at the bottom of the pasture, I experienced a warm, golden light behind me, beaming over my shoulders, warming the back of my neck. I turned around, but there was no vehicle with lights, no source of light at all. We glided seamlessly together in the dark night, arm in arm. Not long after, my right shoulder became warm, and I noticed a golden luster in my peripheral vision. Now I remember it as a living light like small fireflies dancing in a matrix. I looked behind and saw a fading golden glow, breaking up into pixel-like, fading particles, but no source of illumination.

I asked John, striding beside me, "Do you see the light shining behind me?"

"No," he said. "Nothing."

One night the light was so bright it glared all around the back of my body. That time I was certain someone had a strong spotlight turned on me, a hunter or a late-night walker. I turned around quickly to surprise whoever it was, and started running in the direction of the light. No one was there. Sometimes it seemed more than one light, but always the beam shone over my right shoulder, confusing and, somehow, edgy. The light warmed me, but warned me too, being similar in feeling to a light I had once encountered on the North Island.

We had visited Aotearoa for the first time two years earlier, when we reserved a room at a fishing lodge on a lake near Rotorua, far enough away from the city to be in a quiet forest. We arrived quite late off the flight from Los Angeles and didn't reach the lodge until after 9 p.m. Needing to stretch, when we checked in I asked the host where we could find a walking trail. He pointed to a forested knoll across from the lodge, its silhouette Prussian blue in the silver moonlight. He suggested we go straight along the well-marked path, where we would find a route that circled round to come back. He mentioned that the trail passed a Māori cemetery. Ten minutes on the trail took us upward and along a small path, which we navigated slowly in the dim torch light through the tree tunnel in the forest.

I walked around a curve and abruptly stumbled against a sheet of vertical light like a closed door. It was slightly visible; there, but not there. I was surprised. Surely, I had imagined it. I gently tried to continue forward, leaning into it with my shoulders. My body felt a soft gel-like resistance from head to foot. Something prevented me moving forward. I stepped back, and John passed around me, then he quickly stopped too.

"I can't move forward," he said.

At the same moment, we both turned and walked quickly and silently back the way we had come.

At that time, I knew little of the indigenous Māori people, but I imagined them deeply absorbed in land, sea, and sky. Their ancestors were part of the great South Pacific migrations which had peopled an enormous ocean nation. Their sailors read the skies and seas on epic journeys during long apprenticeships with master navigators. These geniuses of nature, the ancestors of New Zealand, would have noticed the beautiful hill sited on the dark, shining lake, shimmering in the night air, and selected it as an appropriate spiritual burial ground. I can still close my eyes and see that densely forested mount, the indigo shadows, and the gentle but firm resistance on the trail. The cemetery was off bounds and guarded; it was tapu, set apart for a consecrated purpose.

We weren't as surprised as we might have been by the paranormal prohibition on the path. Over the past two years, we had been visited by a poltergeist at our small cottage south of Miami, I had seen a ghost in a Victorian flat in London, and a spirit had compressed John's chest in bed. I'd had intense kundalini rushes in meditation, seen auras, and worked with ecstatic body postures in the New Mexican desert. After hours of meditation with seekers of knowledge in Miami, I saw a blazing white/gold light, not a light on the outside, a shining light on the inside when my eyes were closed. There was a sun between my eyebrows that was warm and pumping gold spiraling light. The white/gold light had more intensity than the warm golden light over my shoulder on the riverbank.

Before buying land in Wainui, during the years in Miami, I became acquainted with a young man, Ernesto (Ernie) Pichardo, a fully initiated priest of the West African Yoruba god, Shango. A famous, handsome deity in the Yoruba diaspora, Shango is god of thunder, dance and justice. A king and general, he ended his rule on Earth in self-destruction and resurrection. I was intrigued by the young priest, a Cuban exile in Miami, but I really had no idea what his powers or his training might be. He was nineteen, and I was twenty-seven with a new Ph.D. I had lived in the Yoruba speaking area of Nigeria before moving to Miami. There, I had studied and performed with theater groups, absorbing Yoruba stories until they felt like my own.

Ernie was still a teenager, but was then, and still is, *Obá Oríaté* and *Italero* (Ceremonial Leader and Master Diviner), as well as Shango priest of the Yoruba Lucumí religion. One day, when he visited my university anthropology of religion class, Ernie quietly revealed his predestined life mission and career. He worked with departed spirits.

"Working with spirits is like drinking water to me," he explained.

His phrase summarised a great deal of the difference between the Anglo and the Latino world view in Miami. Even Latinos who were not Lucumí priests, especially Catholics, included the spirit world in their lives, while Anglos, at least at that time, were still obsessed with proving there was one. The barrier on the cemetery trail the night we arrived in Aotearoa, and the lights on the riverbank, were part of the invisible world of spirit around us, intriguing in ways we didn't understand, but perfectly natural in Ernie's world.

Two years after meeting Ernie, John and I bought the land we named Waitaha, which we thought of as our own Garden of Eden. However, after a few years we altered that name to the Yoke of Paradise, because we still lived and worked in Miami over eight thousand miles away. When we were in Miami, we would say, "We have to sell it! It's too much trouble." But then we would return to Wainui, swing around the last bend in the road, see the mountains behind our land full of rainforest, and catch our breath. We couldn't sell Waitaha; the yoke of paradise bound us.

We travelled to New Zealand to work on our land a few weeks, or sometimes months, of the year. During those times we planted native trees, because the scars of farming were not going to heal without help, and we needed insulation from the cattle farm below. When we started the locals thought that only Australian trees, or almost any tree but New Zealand natives, would grow, and that cattle grazing could stop invasive gorse and blackberry. In fact, grazing made invasive plants much worse and harder to remove from the compacted soil, and cows didn't like them. One farmer's wife thought no trees could ever grow on our land again. In our naiveté, we believed this land would grow nothing else as well.

Our land was in the middle of a temperate rainforest park, receding as cattle ate the edges. Nonetheless, the high rainfall and relatively recent clearing of the forest offered a great chance for regrowth of native trees. For a long while we allowed the gorse to grow wild, until it was fourteen feet high with young natives coming up underneath. At the same time, we also planted native trees around the prickly, strong gorse. The theory was that shade kills gorse; throw some shade its way, and it withers slowly, weakens and dies. At that stage there was no hint of this final decline, only its present full-bodied, impenetrable, springing upward. During this time in our county there were immense acreages of gorse where the forest had been burned and the land left fallow.

Our Kiwi neighbours called us "the gorse people" as they debated how our experiment would end: gorse up the mountain and down the valley, thick as my thigh, and unstoppable except with fire and poisons. Instead, our planted trees grew into a small forest where the creeks run clear, birds flourish, and the dairy farm below is invisible. Run the projector at extremely slow speed when you visualise this growth, beginning with the scene of twelve-inch saplings grown in root trainers planted in prickly gorse and blackberry, and in pasture grass bred to withstand anything. Many of the trees died before they were two, lost in the weeds and grass. But enough lived to get above the fray and reach for the Sun. Run that projector forward until you can see, in the middle of the former pasture, the once-thick boles of gorse lying dead in groves where shade prevented further growth. Now imagine a shady grove of kowhai trees or manuka or fern trees on a hot summer day—cool, darkly shaded, with water running in the gullies.

When our planted trees were small, we continued to travel between Miami and Waitaha, so that my husband and I could pursue our careers and see family and friends. During this time, Ernie became my Lucumí *padrino* (godfather). Many times he read my fortune and destiny through the lens of his intelligence, character and experience, while deploying the Cuban/Yoruba oracle called the Dilogún, a symbolic system not unlike the Chinese I Ching. When I became Ernie's godchild, he presented *elekes* to me—necklaces symbolic of the Orisha, the Yoruba spirits/gods of nature and culture. It was natural for Ernie, and an intrinsic part of his religion, to honour plants and trees. He made healing remedies from them, considering them as alive and full of spirit as people.

In fact, the whole body of ancient knowledge in the sacred divination form known as Ifá and the Dilogún were taught to the human world by an ancient tree. My dreams became tangled with trees and Ernie's house. The first time Ernie sent me into the forest on a ritual journey, my spiritual well-being merged with trees. Now it is trees I remember most vividly when I leave a place: their calm beauty, lovely, fresh air atmosphere, and high branches filled with birds. Good smells, leaves gently rustling in the wind, peeling bark, or shiny trunk covered in enigmatic galls that tell a history of interaction with the world.

When I plant a tree, for a few days I feel its roots underground, stretching through the moist brown soil, harmonising with the environment. In a most mysterious way, the sapling is connected to my heart. Italian scientists say that plants and trees are best described as living computers with many senses; trees share and transmit large volumes of information within themselves and with others.[2] I think at some level everyone knows that trees, like rivers and oceans, are ancient healers and the finest medicine. Trees and water harmonise human beings. If you want spiritual happiness, trees, especially those growing near a river or by the ocean, are very good places to find it. Young trees fill you with new oxygen. One day I recovered quickly from carbon monoxide poisoning. While standing in a group of small beech trees about my size, I inhaled deeply and exhaled completely across their young foliage until I felt much better. The whole time I could hear the communion of birds and insects in the branches of parent trees nearby.

I find the longer I spend out-of-doors, the more my life veers away from the mundane. My dreams change. I experience myself turning into the trees, birds, rivers, oceans and mountains, which vibrate with a pervading trill. One summer afternoon in Waitaha, that shimmering vibration overwhelmed my senses with pleasure during this transportation. I simultaneously noticed that green plants and trees were growing, leaves brown and dry were decomposing, seeds were sprouting, blossoms were opening, and my ears were quivering. I was immersed in the buzzing of bees, the clicking of cicadas, and the twittering and peeping of birds hidden in gullies and lost in green canopies. I smiled as I watched bumblebees dive into the lavender hearts of artichoke blooms. They went for heaven, swimming down into the deep violet flowers, their furry little black bums and golden pollen baskets remaining upright like islands in a purple lake. Yet this wonderful natural world is on a steep decline. Sometimes, I try to imagine what the sounds and

---

[2] Stephano Marcuso and Alessandra Viola, *Brilliant Green: The Surprising History and Science of Plant Intelligence*, Island Press, Washington, 2015. There are many books around this theme.

colour were like three hundred years ago. I can't. In 1642, during the few days they were anchored in Wainui Bay, Abel Tasman's sailors asked him to move further off shore because the bird song was keeping them awake.

In the later afternoon, I noticed there was a pause for the world to exhale, as the long twilight seamlessly transformed into evening's deep ultramarine sky, sparkling with stars, satellites and distant ships on the horizon. One by one, all the birds left the trees around the veranda and the weka disappeared into the shrubs. Already, there was water vapor in the air and a katabatic breeze blowing from the forest. I felt like shouting, "No, don't let this perfection end. May this day last forever!"

Then I heard a descant from the tui, whose bell-like song evoked depths of soul and soothed my passion. Soon the drowsing tui was replaced by a now awakened little owl, the morepork, whose haunting cries crowned the enchantment of the night.

Veriditas was a word used by the eleventh century mystic Hildegard von Bingen. Hildegard put the Latin words for green and truth (*viridis* and *veritas*) together in one evocative word, which meant *the omniscient presence of the green force of creation*. That day in my garden I had a deep feeling of veriditas, the ever present One, within every speck of life, always evolving. Veriditas is something sacred, in perpetual motion, the trill that animates and enlightens the ever-changing universe. The Lucumí call this sacred force *ashé*. The afternoon when I thought of nothing else, veriditas didn't stop when I went inside, because it can't stop; it just is, even in my house. My act of observation doesn't change it.

Veriditas is a natural law of the universe. It is *the* mystery. Where did it come from? When did it begin? Why does it exist? Will it ever stop? Trees are one source of wisdom about this sacred energy in perpetual motion. In fact, for those who listen carefully, apparently trees can transfer, from an all-knowing source, universal truths about life which can guide Homo sapiens. I like to remember I am a primate who loves trees. Certainly my ancestors lived in them, long ago. My closest primate relatives still live in them. I can't forget my relations. Jane

Goodall describes the chimps who are her friends at Gombe Reserve when they sit together to marvel at the sunset.

What if trees are meant to be the teachers of Homo sapiens, a primate who left the Garden of Eden and the Tree of Life, because of a made-up story in the apocalyptic land that still threatens our world? Are we "caught in the devil's bargain, and we've got to get ourselves back to the garden", like Joni sang at the Big Sur Folk Festival in 1969, a month after the immortal Woodstock? I feel we are living in a time of chaos because we left our teachers the trees in the forest, and now we have cut most of the ancient forests down. Therefore, it may be our sacred purpose to reforest our Earth and make it healthy again.

Siddhartha transformed into the Buddha when he accepted the wisdom and shelter of the Bodhi tree. In Lucumí tradition, an ancient Mother Tree taught Ifá divination, and its body of enlightenment knowledge, to the divine child Orúnmìlà while he was buried under her enormous canopy. This Mother Tree's knowledge has been translated through the ages by Yoruba diviners like Ernie. It was Ernie who showed me how to begin a simple spiritual practice with trees and ancestral spirit guides. I've practised divination with Tarot cards and I Ching shells, for myself and others, for two decades. These practices have taken me deeper into Wainui and its landscapes, spirits, stories, ancestors—and into myself. Now I want to take you with me a little deeper into Waitaha.

When I last saw Ernie in Miami, just two months before writing this, he advised me that I must speak about the indigenous ancestors of my home in Waitaha. They must be acknowledged as part of the setting for the natural landscape and the Māori prophecy that unfolded on the Wainui riverbank a few years ago.

The last Māori chief of Wainui was a member of a tribe from Te Ika-a-Māui, the North Island. His tribe was allied with others. They settled our area at the top of Te Waipounamu in the nineteenth century and lived through very difficult times. Their people stand out in New Zealand colonial history as receiving brutal treatment. In laying a foundation for understanding the last chief of Wainui, I speak both from research and intuition; the same for the taniwha, an archetypal figure of great fascination, and for Tāne Mahuta, the tree who gave birth to humanity.

2. WAITAHA ANCESTORS

The South Island countryside with its mahinga kia³ had provided Ngai Tahu with their traditional prosperity. When this land passed into European hands the runholders grew rich and became the new aristocracy of Te Wai Pounamu, while Ngai Tahu grew poor and lived like outcasts.

— Te Wai Pounamu Harry Evison

THE FIRST YEAR WE LIVED on our land, Waitaha, my husband and I built our small, off-the-grid home. By night-time we were exhausted, and I rapidly learned new respect for builders. I found the whole process much harder than writing a doctoral dissertation, but the good news was my muscles were outstanding. Faded photos of me wearing a tool belt and T-shirt show my new biceps and strong neck. I'd had no idea my neck could become muscly.

However, while our simple home was growing I had little time to understand the landscape around me. In free moments I visited the ocean, the path on the hillside, the mountain tops, the beaches and estuary. I was captivated when I noticed a sign at Wainui Bay informing me that Māori had once lived near the headland. The small sign also posed a question I couldn't stop thinking about: *Kei te noho a Taupo i raro i te ra. Kei hea nga tangata whenua?* Taupo lives beneath the Sun. Where are the people of the past? Where, indeed? I hadn't the faintest idea.

I was aware of Māori culture. Before visiting New Zealand for the first time I had read *Teacher* by Sylvia Ashton Warner. But my research

---

³ Ngai Tahu's traditional tribal food sources.

was in West Africa, northern Quebec and Miami, and I had no formal training in Māori studies. Warner had taught Māori children to read using their own inner visions, children who could catch their lunch in the ocean. For a long time, I couldn't answer the questions, "What is New Zealand like?" or "Who are New Zealanders?" Nothing reminded me of a culture where the indigenous people left school at lunch to catch lobsters in the sea. I had seen children do that in Fiji, but nothing like it in Wainui, which has white farmers and their children, all with a British heritage. I had no idea where the Māori were. We had bought our land for the Tahitian-like mountains around it, the river and waterfall beside it, and the ocean in the middle distance. It was also remarkably inexpensive, like many things in those days. We knew we would have to reforest it, but, luckily, we had no idea what that meant.

For many years, I only knew the Pākehā[+] farmers, whose own culture was truncated through isolation from their homeland in the British Isles. None knew anything of substance about the Māori people who had lived in Wainui before them or of their own ancestral homes in England and Scotland. Their knowledge of New Zealand history started and stopped with their own grand and great grandparents' immigration and settling. Their schools taught European history, and they told family stories to their clans.

At that time, the traditional farming population held onto the notion that New Zealand was a white country discovered for their benefit. When Ernie said the ancestors of Wainui must appear in this story, I didn't initially think about the white people as ancestors, although many Pākehā families had come and gone. The desire to escape learning about the reality of colonialism, which I hadn't thought existed in New Zealand, was tempting me into not looking into the age of conquest. The local story line around Māori/Pākehā relations was that Māori people hadn't suffered like their counterparts, the Indians in North America and Aboriginals in Australia. When I became friends with a Māori woman, Aroha, I got a reality check. She and her family

---

[+] The word Pākehā now refers to white people and also to all non-Māori people.

had suffered a great deal. I learned more as time passed.

That was decades ago. Much has changed, although as this story unfolds you will see that the human, environmental and spiritual legacy of the colonisation of New Zealand by the British is still present. Today, when I hear people talk about the ancestors, it is in a Māori context. Like many indigenous people, Māori honour their ancestors with ceremonies and prayers, offerings and altars. But in understanding the landscape of Wainui, the first question I needed to ask, because it was monumentally obvious, was how the dairy industry had replaced the temperate rainforest and extensive wetlands. The people who achieved this transformation were the white ancestors of Wainui.

The nineteenth to the early twentieth century was the time of colonialisation, which ruled with guns and laws, had a more powerful god, spread strange diseases, and was greedy for timber and gold. British natural resources at home were nearly exhausted, but they had the fire power, the big boats, and the wealth to finance exploratory missions to obtain more resources from other parts of the world, including here in Aotearoa. Today, planting a flag and saying, "This is my King's land now", is the stuff of late-night comedy. But when His Majesty's flagpole and flag were erected on shorelines throughout the Pacific, and elsewhere around the world, those lands were being claimed under British law. On the North Island of New Zealand, Captain Cook sent a small boat to shore to do this, not even stepping on the land he was claiming for Britain.

Wainui and the bays around it were nearly empty when white settlers arrived, yet prior to that they were continuously populated by Māori living in villages with fortified hill forts called pa. Judging by the number of artefacts and sites along the coast, Wainui at one time accommodated several lively villages, offered fertile land for growing kumara and potatoes, and its seas provided mammoth numbers of fish, shellfish, and birds to many people. Despite that, the whole South Island was declared *terra nullius* (nobody's land) in 1840 by Lieutenant William Hobson, under instruction from the British Government, allowing British political occupation and protection of the Crown's rights. Can you imagine saying, "These tribes aren't Christian, they are heathens, therefore the land is unoccupied, and I claim this whole island for my Christian monarch."? On the other hand, maybe it's not so surprising today; when I look at the politics of my country of birth, the USA, I appreciate Homo sapiens are capable of anything.

So, the British got a new country, and eventually they arrived with surveying equipment in Wainui. Imagine how wonderful Aotearoa's forests looked to these colonisers. The forests were vast, the trees straight and tall, and the wood could make incredible masts and buildings. Britain and Scotland had lost their old trees a long time before. In 1905, when Wainui was being settled by white colonists, England had only a little over five percent of its forest left. In Scotland, only one percent of its famous pinelands remained, and wild animals were being hunted to extinction. Their disappearance caused little disappointment for the working person, because during the nineteenth century in both countries the King and large land holders owned and managed all the hunting animals. Norman laws, imposed in England after the conquest in 1066, created royal forests where the English were forbidden to hunt. These forests were privately enclosed by the seventeenth century. Richard the Lion Hearted could have your eyes gouged out for killing one of his deer; two fingers were chopped off for a rabbit. Indeed, when immigrants reached New Zealand, it had been a long time since they had been allowed to fell a tree or hunt their dinner without risk of losing a body part.

Our first white farmers in Wainui were from the British Isles. Before settling here it's likely none of them would have had a tree to cut or an animal to hunt and kill. They were not British royalty, and had little education or resources. However, they were ready to be royalty on their own land, which was what the New Zealand Company, formed to sell New Zealand cheaply to settlers, had on offer. Settler farmers were given every advantage by the new government, and did, by the twentieth century, end up like New Zealand's royalty. Today, forgetting their own hungry origins in the British Isles, the worst offense possible for Wainui farmers is to find that a poacher has been hunting on their land. I haven't seen any gouged-out eyes or missing fingers, but fists have flown.

The dairy farmers I met when I first arrived in Wainui were the grandsons of the early white settlers. They had lovely western-style homes, big verandas, rooms for many children, barns and milking sheds built with views of the water and surrounding mountains. Derelict cottages, which the farmer's grandparents had built, were scattered in the hills and bays, each with its own narrative to be discovered. The oldest cottage, a small wooden shack in a bay near Wainui, was a walk over the hill away. It was set on a river estuary, a gorgeous spot. The cottage had one main room, with no indoor sink or water, and was dominated by an open fire that extended across most of one wall. There was a second, much smaller room. Before visiting, I learned that a family of eight had lived there. As I walked around the tiny space, I kept thinking that when the children were teenagers they must have built small huts outside for sleeping. There were torn papers everywhere, old shoes turning into earth, and newspaper articles from early in the twentieth century. I found the remnants of a flour sack, and a tea cannister from Hong Kong.

A breeze blew through the shack because it was falling down and disappearing. It had been built close to a river tributary flowing into an enormous estuary. The vibration of water was everywhere, and I wondered how this delicate shack had remained standing when the river flooded. A small school had been built near the river's bend for children from the newly arrived families. There they kept sheep and cows, and practised wood cutting and flax milling, for as long as those resources lasted. However, after the forests were burned down, the land on the sloping hills quickly lost fertility and people left.

I couldn't imagine how hard a woman had to work in that wee cottage to provide meals, clean, wash, mend, and make clothes, keep a garden, gather firewood, keep water boiling on the fire, give birth, raise children, tend sick kids and animals, grow a garden, make soap and candles, scones and preserves, and so much more—no doubt my list is short and naïve. The woman of that cottage had one open fire in a handmade stone fireplace with a metal arm to hang a cooking pot. No refrigeration. A shelf or two for storage. She endured the clearing and burning of the forest, coping with soot and ashes flying everywhere, responding to the coming of the herding animals and all that meant for her husband, while she had child after child. For a long time, the landscape was like a war zone around the woman, its destruction assured because its enemy, working with metal tools, fires, saws and mills, dreamed of transforming the land into a new-world Britain.

Dreams are illusions until they are made real. I've seen photos of the cottage with a woman in a long Victorian skirt, wearing a blouse with lace collar and a large brooch, her hair in a tidy chignon. Her family are around her, dressed in special photo attire, including very white shirts on the boys and men. The cottage behind them is small, and there is a view of the hills and land around it. It would be an ordinary family photo from that era, except that the photo was taken after the apocalypse. The woman sits on a kitchen chair, looking away from the black, scorched soil. But we can see around the cottage, and in the far distance, blackened match sticks that stand up like dark and slender stalactites. Not long before they had been trees. That black death was all I could see in the photo, up and down the hills, and across the land near the cottage.

Quite soon after I arrived, someone suggested I read a memoir called *Wainui Bay*, which was in the local library.[5] The writer, Maurice Robertson, was the son of one of the first white settlers of Wainui, was Uncle Maurice to a large number of nieces and nephews, and would have known the family in the cottage. I have twice read Maurice's little work, and each time have been impressed with two things: his description of the magnificent natural environment the family found when they arrived and how joyful it made them, and his contrasting description of the tough, bullying environment among himself and his brothers in their new paradise. When they weren't chopping the forest or flax, making fence posts, tending cows, or milling wood, they were hunting, shooting deer and wild pigs. One son shot the shags on the river because

---

[5] Maurice Robertson, *Wainui Bay*, 1972, Takaka Library, reference copy.

they were eating baby trout. Slowly, through the brothers' and the father's work and play, the original ecosystem was destroyed.

The family had previously lived in a barren place, renting, then purchasing one thousand acres in Wainui Bay from the last Māori chief. Maurice described the small clear streams through heavy forest—a sight they had never seen before—as they made their way along the narrow track to Wainui. Everywhere they saw giant rata trees, and beehives with exposed honey. He mentioned towering kahikatea, giants of the forest, sometimes ninety feet tall before their branches began. Glow worms were everywhere in the forest. The family caught never-ending shoals of whitebait by the gallons as they came up the river; once they speared eighty-two flounders in two hours using a burning rata torch. Tens of thousands of kākā (native parrots) came for three weeks to drink nectar from the rata morning and night. The multitudes of wild creatures he depicted took my breath away. Now there are just a handful of kahikatea, glow worms in only a few places, and whitebait is nearly extinct. We are lucky to see one or two kākā flying overhead, and crayfish are scarce unless you have a boat and know where to go. The bottom of the bay is dead, according to fishermen who have lived here all their lives. By contrast, Maurice reported that herring had come up the river in millions—*they could ride horses through them.*

All of the brothers' games involved killing, hurting and hunting. The crueller the incident—like a spur which sent an old cow running and resulted in a horse being kicked viciously in the ribs—the funnier the story was to Maurice and his brothers. They once spent two hours chopping down an old rata tree just to get the part of the trunk containing honey. In his language everything was broken, burned, cut or killed. The bullocks were broken into the harness to use as a haulage team to take out timber. The men cut the trees and burned the land to pasture their new herds. They also let wild and domestic pigs breed together and inhabit the hills, animals that were destructive to the native landscape, and are still a problem today.

When they cut the trees, they started on the kahikateas first, just across the river from the mill. These were wetland trees whose towering height and girth were the homes for many birds and orchids. They were the trees that bound the wetland, made the river bank strong and biodiverse, hosted many plants, and nurtured wildlife. Water birds bred around them, and fruit eaters loved their berries. Adding to the impressive list, the kahikateas clarified water as it flowed back out to the estuary and sea, an important part of the hydrological cycle. Today, a tiny fragment remains of this great forest. A drain gathers its water and carries it off, so one day even this will be no more. While the forest remained, the Scots family carried 10,000 feet of timber at a time out of Wainui for settlers' homes. It would have taken 6,500 feet of board timber to build a 1,000 square foot home; every day, the brothers and their father cut enough timber from Wainui to build at least one home for a new British settler in Christchurch, where most orders were shipped. It only took a few years to cut down the temperate rainforest.

I was at our home in Waitaha a few months after we had built it, lying in our small upstairs loft under the rafters. John was in Miami, where I would join him in a few days. Lying on my back, looking up at the macrocarpa rafters and ceiling, a golden colour with many veins and designs, I was proud of the job we had done. I was breathing with slow rhythmic breaths, letting my eyes move slightly out of focus. As I gazed upward, I saw the figure of a woman from the early twentieth century hovering over me. She was probably forty-five years old, her dark hair pulled severely away from her face. She was wearing a light blue pinafore with darker stripes and floral patterning, had on a blouse with plain short sleeves under the pinafore, and she was thin, but not skinny.

The woman appeared as clear as a projected image on a screen. I wondered if I should be afraid, as I often am when these things happen. But, for once, I remained still and calm. About my size, she stayed above me while I studied her carefully for a minute or so, allowing me to gain a strong impression of the woman before her image faded. I felt she had worked really hard in her life in the house that once existed where we built our new one. She was very solemn and quiet, unemotional and resigned. We had found old bricks that had been a fireplace, fallen in a heap under a mat of grass. We knew this was the kitchen of the house, which may have burned down around 1930, according to the older Wainui farmer who had played around the place as a child. Those same bricks were now a surround for our wood stove. She and I had both touched the bricks; I was connected to the spirit in the pinafore through them. For those moments I looked back at history. It reminded me there was no record of a woman in Maurice's memoir; in passing, he only briefly mentioned his sister and mother.

Another account of Wainui exists, written by a woman who would have lived near here around the time of the woman in the pinafore. Bessie O'Connor was an amateur archaeologist living here in the early twentieth century. She spent her time rambling along the coastline and up the rivers, where she found many, many artefacts—"curios" she called them—of the Māori tribes who had inhabited the area for centuries. She was surprised by the large number of them, and that they were especially easy to find up the rivers. I think I would get along with Bessie, and I love these words of hers written in her own hand: "Here, where the Māori worked for the love of it, shall we, in the lust of acquisition, work ourselves into a sweat digging up his bones? Sacrilege is no name of it!"[6]

In Bessie's day, like our own, there was no end to the monetisation of the landscape. Bessie was disgusted with farmers who once regarded Māori stone tools and other artefacts with disdain, relics of a savage tribe. Now those same farmers, aware of their value on home and foreign markets, had begun to dig them up to sell to visitors. Bessie was right to think that in the future the wonderfully formed stone artefacts, especially those made of greenstone, the coveted pounamu from the west coast of Te Waipounamu, would be worth more than the British metal tools.

---

[6] *The Māori in the Landscape*. Bessie O'Connor nee Winter was a relation of the Hadfields at Awaroa, a bay and valley not far from Wainui. These notes are in her own hand and are over a hundred years old, according to Mr. W. Hadfield of Awaroa. Thanks to Jim Robertson for sharing these notes with me.

Bessie observed many shell middens on her long walks along the coastline, and I also saw that villages had left their shells in a midden or two on the coast of Wainui Bay. Where there was erosion along the coast remains of a midden poured out onto the beach. Pipi, cockle and mussel shells were thick in the sand. Who were the people who had left the beautiful stone tools and decorative items in the land, and dined expansively on seafoods? We know there were at least four Māori tribes living one after the other in Wainui, stretching back six hundred years. The Māori practised conquest and migration. Those few Māori people still living in Wainui during Bessie's time were called the Ngāti Tama. Recently, I became acquainted with a Ngāti Tama ancestor, Chief Paramena, who lived in the nineteenth century in Wainui Bay.

With that acquaintanceship, a new view of Waitaha materialised for me, one that existed before Bessie, the woman on my ceiling, or the other white settlers.

3. CONVERSATIONS WITH THE CHIEF

Oh, chiefs of old!
Ye have vanished from us like the moa bird,
That ne'er is seen of man.
O, lordly totara tree!
Thou'rt fallen to the earth,
And nought but worthless shrubs are left.
—A funeral song of the Ngāti Toa and Ngāti Raukawa

WAINUI HAD VERY EARLY MĀORI settlements and landing docks, built over six centuries, long before either the arrival of the Ngāti Tama, Chief Paramena's tribe, or the British. I had no idea there was a record of the life of this chief who lived in Wainui with his people, starting with the long paddle by waka that brought him as a boy. But there is.[7] Furthermore, his daughter Rangi, who died in Wainui at fourteen, probably of a European disease like measles or mumps, lies a forty-minute walk from my home that begins along the river and ends on the riverside urupā (burial place) where Rangi's headstone stands.

Chief Paramena travelled to Wainui on a heke, a voyage of settlement, and was living there prior to 1841 when the New Zealand Company arrived on the north of the South Island seeking more land. A young boy, he had voyaged with his father, brothers, and cousins on

---

[7] Hilary and John Mitchell, *Te Tau Ihu O Te Waka, Vol IV,* Huia Press, 2014, pgs. 70-76. Throughout this chapter I use their work, except where it is obvious the information comes from my own insights and divinations. Any mistakes are mine, not theirs.

thirteen waka from the Ngāti Tama iwi. I can picture those long craft in the mountainous swells of the straits as they crossed between islands. After that, they had the long journey across the top of the South Island, where they finally paddled around the Wainui headland. There, they landed at a village site that had existed long before the Ngāti Tama and their allies had captured it a few years earlier in order to create space for their clans. When the paddlers reached Wainui Bay, they found native forest and flax, abundant birds, a sea full of fish and a river full of eels. There was good sun and land for cultivation.

Paramena and his whānau probably inhabited flax huts left by the previous occupants, while building strong new homes of their own from the wondrous sea of flax in Wainui. They would have established fishing grounds and dug gardens for potato and kumara cultivation. The plenty of Wainui supplied their food needs. There were extensive pipi and cockle beds, mussels over the rocks, and endless fish, sharks and crayfish. However, this paradisiacal situation ended with the arrival of the surveyor.

The paddlers had left their homeland north of Taranaki because white colonists had taken their land. The New Zealand Company in London had designed a "systematic colonisation" policy to overwhelm Māori land ownership. The drive for land was relentless. Paramena remembered the New Zealand company's arrival in Tasman in 1841, and the arrival of the first settlers when he was thirteen. After that, it was only six years until the arrival of Donald Sinclair, a resident magistrate based in Nelson, the small colonial town just around the bay from Wainui. Sinclair appraised Wainui's resources for colonial settler-farmers and organized surveyors, whose lines, some made with pencil on brown paper, would determine their lives from that time on. Chief Paramena did not have a peaceful life in Wainui. Within a few years after the Ngāti Tama's arrival in Wainui, everything had changed.

By 1861, James Mackay, the district's autocratic colonial administrator, reported, "The Natives of Wainui move backwards and forwards between there and Takaka; they have a fair quantity of land under crop. They are not generally liked by Europeans, as they are in the habit of blustering and bounding. Their chief Paramena is, for a Māori, a wealthy man."[8]

"Blustering and bounding" meant Māori stood up for their rights. Paramena was not a wealthy man, except in land parcels that he owned in Wainui as a result of responding to new white land laws as positively as he could. When they offered to sell some crown land back to Māori people—an ironic recognition that they had taken so much land Māori could not live—Paramena bought it, perhaps with money earned on the gold fields. But these parcels had to support his extended family. They were very small compared to what the iwi might have laid claim to communally a hundred years earlier, when products of ocean, forest and land were managed and shared, and people grew potatoes to trade to visiting ships in return for iron tools.

New white laws designated ownership over everything. The early generosity of the Māori toward the whites changed because, while the whites enriched themselves, Māori became poorer and poorer and found themselves owning less and less land. In 1862, the people of Wainui, including Chief Paramena, were still complaining about boundaries of the reserves that the New Zealand Company and the Crown had arbitrarily surveyed across their lands. It is no wonder that the poor working-class immigrant from the British Isles felt he had inherited the Earth. The New Zealand Company pressed for more and more land for the farmers, and smaller and smaller reserves for Māori, who also had to learn a wholly new language just to protest. There were national confiscations across New Zealand. Our landscape and history in Wainui reflect a local version of the shrinking Māori culture and estate. Paramena held onto his land until 1902, when he leased his thousand acres to the Scots family. He was too old and poor and had no living children, making it impossible for him to survive financially in the new money economy.

I look back on those events and think about Paramena. When I want to feel his presence, I enjoy walking to his daughter Rangi's grave,

---

[8] Mitchell, H.& J, *Te Tau Ihu O Te Waka*, p. 75, from a notebook of MacKay's.

where I have the impression of contact with her and her father. This morning, I walked there just after dawn, and found the river water a blue mirror radiating light across Rangi's headstone. Her grave is on a low bluff next to the estuary, nestled by fern and low hanging branches, and surrounded with a small wrought iron fence. The lovely edge of her urupā is a necklace of small trees along the water.

As I stepped towards her resting place, two kererū flew out of the trees overhead and skimmed over her gravestone before gliding through the opening in the forest. Their opalescent colours flashed in the sunlight, and their wings made a distinctive creaking as they glided out of the forest and over the sea. It was an excellent omen that welcomed my visit. I felt comfortable and at home. The soft sea air was sensual. I wanted to stretch out on the ground and not leave. I lay the offerings I had brought for Rangi on her grave; then I talked to her. I felt entranced as I watched the estuary current flow gently in front of the urupā while the Sun sparkled madly on the water's surface. I don't know if he is buried near his daughter by the sea, but Chief Paramena was there in spirit. I had a tingling feeling of excitement as I concentrated on emptying my mind.

When I returned home, I went immediately to my divination temple and, using shells and cards, asked Paramena if he would speak with me. His first answer was, "Today is a day of grace and synergy, light on light." This was an excellent sign.

I asked him about the driving force of his life in Wainui. His answer surprised me in its obviousness. I guess I expected him to say something about the Māori political situation.

"Whānau," he repeated several times. Family. Of course.

His family was most important to him. They were the people related to him, who lived beside him, worked with him, prayed with him, and who suffered with him. Family was the reason he had journeyed from Te Ika-a-Māui when he was a boy to find a new homeland in Wainui. The boy grew into a chief who became the centre of his family, his goodness or his evil radiating from him and defining his Ngāti Tama community. He had to do well for them. His own life, his own ego, did not matter. Family was why he went long distances to the Māori land court to testify about lineage and boundaries, and why he struggled constantly with the new laws and language in his efforts to retain land in Wainui. Everything was done so his family in Wainui might retain some land.

In the North Island, despite Māori protests and actions against the confiscations of Ngāti Tama and their allies' land, the British had pushed on through the Ngāti Tama homeland of Taranaki, where they took more and more flat land for their settlers. After the Māori protests, the British confiscated even more land to "repay" the Crown for their military expenses during the defeat of Parihaka, the largest Māori village in Taranaki. Then, although his daughter and homeland in Taranaki were gone, and his land in Wainui was threatened by new laws and taxes, Chief Paramena still had to function for his Wainui whānau, which needed his leadership to survive.

Paramena spoke further in my divination. "I watched our land getting smaller, and I had to agree with whatever the invaders said, because when I didn't they did it anyway. My family was small and getting sick, and no woman could keep her tamariki (child) alive for very long. The whites had brought evil with them in the form of illnesses no tohunga (traditional healer and priest) could cure. The walls of the mountains were closing on us."

This is why, before Paramena's death, he leased his land to the Scots family, who eventually bought it from him. After his death, according to Maurice, the Scots brothers resided in a superbly built whare erected by a Māori. They feasted on peaches from an old Māori orchard, and found Māori traps for catching kākās (native parrots). Scotland and its food shortages, poor labour conditions, crowded cities, and freezing winters were a long way away.

Paramena fell on very hard times in old age. In 1899, a cousin sought financial assistance for him from the Public Trustee, who held the income from the Nelson Tenths Reserves, rentals of Māori land to white colonists. Paramena was seventy-eight years old at this time, but help was declined. Paramena and his two brothers, Riwai and Parau, died without descendants. Paramena died around 1902. He was impoverished, having received no help from the Government or the white people who had leased and bought his land very inexpensively.⁹

A few years later, Bessie and her family arrived in Wainui, where she began searching for the artefacts that once had been real tools for the generations of Māori who had lived in the nearby bays. Not long after that, the white farmers began to tell stories of Wainui from their points of view. For instance, when I first arrived in Wainui, I heard that Paramena was a "devious, crafty old man" who had "murdered his wife" and who boasted of "eating white women." Hillary Mitchell, who has seen the detailed law records kept from this time, believes a murder could not have been committed without being documented, and it had been decades since the Māori had eaten their enemies. However, I do think the threat of being consumed by your enemy could be very effective in establishing distance and respect. Paramena was one of those Māori the locals didn't like because he stood up for his rights. He survived for a while in the Pākehā world by figuring it out, law by law, and protesting: "blustering and bounding".

The last Māori chief of Wainui was on the mind of the Scots family farmer, grandson of the original settler, when he accompanied Hilary and John Mitchell, the extraordinary researchers of *Te Tau Ihu O Te Waka*, to the land where, he informed them, he had established a national treasure, a Queen Elizabeth Trust, on the site of Paramena's last home, the place called "deep hole", where other Ngāti Tama lived beside him. The Mitchells walked around the field near the river while the farmer pointed out the location of Paramena's last home, then climbed up to the urupā, recorded in a lovely photo in their book. I was surprised when I read that statement about a covenant, as my husband and I have a Queen Elizabeth Trust covenant on our land, and we know the other covenanters in our county. I visited the farmer and asked him if he had placed a covenant on Paramena's home by the river. "No," he

---

⁹ Mitchell, H & J, p 76.

said loudly. He repeated it twice. The QE2 says he never phoned or emailed: there is no covenant.[10]

The new farmer has nearly completely filled in the spot where Paramena's "deep hole" would have been, obliterating any trace of Paramena that may have remained. He rides over that spot on his tractor, spreading tons of sand on the land where Paramena's whare and kainga, his settlement was likely to have been. The Mitchells say they are "puzzled", but their memories are clear from that day when the previous farmer showed them the historied land where Paramena had lived. They have no idea how they got it so wrong in their book. Meanwhile, the farmer has no memory of the day. It was another answer for me to the question, "Where are the people of the past?"

After this sad history, I wondered how Paramena would summarise his life in Wainui. I felt resentment and anger that Wainui's ancient trees had been toppled for gain and dairy, and that the Māori who had lived here either died or had to leave because of impoverishment, without a memorial to their existence. I felt nostalgia for a culture I had never known, and sorrow for the Māori community's growing losses. I thought it would be natural for Paramena to feel infuriated and wrathful. I held a divination session in which I concentrated deeply until I felt in touch with Paramena, then asked him to describe how he felt about the colonial toppling not just of the Ngāti Tama in Wainui, but of Māori all over New Zealand.

"There was nothing we could do at this stage, and therefore the principle of submission spread around the country, from Taranaki to Te Urewera to Wainui. We were tied up in a bag, and unable to act."

Did he hate the Pākehā?

"That doesn't enter into it," he said at once through the shells. "From long ago, we learned not to blame heaven or Earth or other

---

[10] Page 77 describes the area where the Mitchell's were told the QE2 covenant was located. There is no covenant and there is nothing in the QE2 files to say they were ever contacted. It would have been a great thing if Paramena had been honored this way because there is so much Māori history in Wainui.

people. We fought and lost. Eventually, with the Pākehā, we adopted non-violence, because we could not win with violence. Through all of this I learned not to be attached to outcomes. Another lesson was 'have patience'. But, please, always remember that when one thing arrives, another departs. This was a natural cycle for us Ngāti Tama."

One thing arrives and another departs, in an eternal cycle. I couldn't argue with that. What a great way to lessen strong feelings about the matter. While I was surprised he didn't want to rant, I definitely could see the results of patience for the Māori people throughout New Zealand, where many iwi have negotiated settlements of some substance. For instance, after seven years of sit-ins on what was formerly Department of Conservation land, the Whanganui River is back in the hands of the iwi from whom my godson is descended. When I was last in Whanganui, local iwi members were still sitting on the banks of the river in the town itself, patiently waiting for the government to hear them about a land claim, this year or next. Perhaps one day the river will run clear and be full of eels again. My godson's relatives say they have the patience to wait as long as it takes.

What did Paramena think about Wainui still losing trees to dairy, a wetland constantly drained for pasture, the paddocks converted to spreading feed lots like Kansas, with not a tree interrupting the line of vision? While Māori horticulturalists had fired large acreages of forest to grow potatoes and cultivate bracken fern which was a food staple, the Pākehā farmers quickly reduced the forest cover to less than ten percent of the original and put grazing animals on the land which assured rapid erosion in hilly areas, along riverbanks, and at the forest's edge. It was fast and brutal, from around 1880-1920, when the extermination of the Māori was a foregone conclusion among colonial government officials.

Here, Paramena's view was quite straightforward and based on Māori tradition: "This is a time of hardship and hindrance. The strange thing that I see is so little accumulation of resources on the land and sea. Everything is shaved clean as if the world can live without the ngahere (forest). We are all descended from Tāne (lord of the forest), and our renewal is dependent on his. Look, even Tāne's great trees on Te Ika-a-

Māui are dying in your time. Soon the spirit of the forest will be gone. Great blessings accumulate around those people who are planting trees again and standing up for the forest."

Those who stand up for the forest. The little forest that remains here in Wainui is in a park and contrasts strongly with the pasture that pushes against it. When I walk on the riverbank as twilight turns to night, the breeze from the waterfall freshens the air with cool wafts from the damp, fertile rainforest upriver, and I know that this breeze refreshed Paramena and his daughter Rangi. When this gentle katabatic wind descends, it moves in the valley like a living presence rather than a chilly breeze. The forest substance beguiles my every pore, just as it must have for thousands of years for the ever-changing cast of inhabitants in Wainui. Green and vibrant, filled with trees, damp moss and clear water, it is pure veriditas, and it doesn't care a whit who lives in the valley. Homo sapiens all look alike to nature.

On evenings like this, my euphoria remains until I become conscious of an acrid smell underlying the forest's pure aromas, a smell emanating from the nearby pasture where three hundred cows graze. For me, this olfactory experience, attars of rainforest mingled with cattle waste, symbolizes the profound difference between a forest and a paddock, freedom and corporate bondage, beauty and foulness, indigenous and colonial. The forest is emerald, chartreuse, shiny with dew; it pulsates with giant yellow-green fronds, towers of epiphytes, grey-white boles thick to a hundred feet high beside the sweet river falling down in noisy rapids over granite stones. This opulence exists just beyond the farmer's fence where, by contrast, unpleasant (no one sits on it, even the cows don't lie on it) closely cropped, damp grass and brown mud, mucked over with dung piles and urine puddles, cradle three hundred lactating cows engaged in making milk powder for distant Chinese children. When the river path enters the forest from this pasture, I feel like a door on the Tardis has opened on Planet Avatar. The long branches high overhead covered with small ferns and long red blooms, dripping soft rain, thrill me in ways I can't describe.

When I talked to Paramena at his urupā the second time, bell birds sang as never before, weaving their mystic melody through my thoughts. I heard them, as if in confirmation of Paramena's spirit's presence, and felt pure joy. Later, in divination, Paramena repeated twice what he says is the foremost point of this book:

Our natural state in nature is joy, and we come to it through the forest and the birds. Innocence and truth are qualities on the path through the forest to find joy.

4. I AM THE MOUNTAIN

I have become an aged ose tree,
I will no longer die.
I have become 200 hills rolled into one.
I am immovable.

— Oracle of Ifa

WHEN I FIRST ARRIVED IN WAINUI, I was told by a farmer that just after his family had arrived, the remaining Māori had climbed into their canoes and paddled away, but he didn't know where. A local Māori knew the answer. After Paramena died, the Māori had paddled back to Taranaki on Te Ika-a-Māui. It left me wondering how they had maintained the vision of their homeland after being away for decades, not to speak of the fitness of the remaining old people who departed. I guess they were paddling throughout their lives, and those who returned had survived European diseases and the loss of their ancestral homeland. As to how they had remembered Taranaki, yesterday I found out at a party here in Golden Bay.

The sky and water were clear and blue, so we gathered on the veranda of our hosts' home. From there we were able to see Mt. Taranaki across the water on the North Island. The sacred mountain shimmered behind filmy streaks of cloud, its magnificent cone well-defined. It looked like it was close and accessible, not the long drive across the top of the South Island, the ferry ride to Wellington, and then five or six more hours by car to get to New Plymouth that it takes today. I hadn't

I AM THE MOUNTAIN 49

realised its visual proximity until I saw Mt. Taranaki's volcanic cap directly across the Cook Straits.

I appreciated on a day like this, Paramena could have beheld his inspiring ancestral mountain, his tupuna maunga, the spiritual identity of his people. Ngāti Tama identity was merged with the mountain, and the sight of the mountain kept the dream current of recovering their homeland. When I saw the stirring sight of Taranaki's beauty on the horizon, I decided I also would have paddled back there if I had been left in Wainui when the resources and land were gone. I have learned from Māori culture and the story of Chief Paramena that I am the mountain, the river and the land. The tangata whenua are people who are part of the landscape, the land, and the water.

There are messages in my day which help me remember my deep evolutionary connection to the mountain. For instance, in the mornings, my yoga routine begins with a posture called tadasana, the mountain. This is the primary standing posture that opens a sequence in which I gain strength, balance and flexibility. Tadasana reminds me of the Māori mihi, words of formal introduction and greeting which are used in many situations. I learned them in the language course *Te Ataarangi*. Designed to teach everyone a mihi in a few hours, it is remarkably effective in helping Pākehā integrate their identities into the Māori world. When introducing oneself, like many Māori people, one may use the mountain that is closest to home as a part of personal identity. Nearly every range and prominent peak in Aotearoa is linked to local tribal identity and mana. Special reverence is given to the higher peaks such as Tongariro, Ruapehu, Taranaki and Hikurangi in the North Island, or Aoraki in the South Island. A Māori proverb states: Mehemea ka tuohu ahau me maunga teitei. If I should bow my head let it be to a high mountain.[11] I try to recall this whakatauki when I am standing in tadasana and my mind devolves to petty concerns.

I glance outside my window to the mountains, which are not

---

[11] Andy Dennis, *Mountains: People and mountains*, in *Te Ara, the Encyclopaedia of New Zealand*, http://www.TeAra.govt.nz/en/mountains/page-5.

moving despite the high gales and thunder. I would like to be the same, unmoved by chaotic forces, immune to the dark challenges of Pluto and Uranus, the gods of rapid, often upsetting and challenging transformation. When I am in tadasana, I visualize myself as a mountain, a being which cannot be moved except by a great natural force like an earthquake or volcanic eruption. In my yoga practice, my mind is the equivalent of an eruption, and it can knock me over when I lose focus. Literally, I will fall out of tadasana, or any posture, when the worries of the day overwhelm my thoughts, and I lose control. Suddenly, I am wobbling and compensating for my lack of balance in the mountain pose, and I find myself in a quake rocking left and right. Lack of balance is the foremost negative quality in our world today.

> We have become unstable for various reasons. Today it seems that we are without roots, without a genuine connection to where we have come from, to where we are in the moment, and to where we are headed in the future. Allowing ourselves to connect to the deep-seated origins that existed thousands of years before us brings healing at a profound mystical level.[12]

As my spine extended this morning in tadasana, my head felt lighter and my feet coupled me to the Earth, stabilising and supporting. I felt my crown on the mountain's peak and my body, the mass of earth, unmoving but alive. Tadasana becomes the physical, mental, and spiritual image of a balanced life when I merge with a mountain in the posture. This is a physical example of what the archetype of the mountain can do when it is summoned.

Collectively, the mountain represents the same archetype for iwi who, through their whakapapa, their genealogies, link people to a mountain in kinship. In a way, through this affinity, the iwi members have supernatural genes that emanate from Mt. Taranaki. These are their "deep-seated origins". The homeland cannot be forgotten because

---

[12] Judith Harris, *Jung and Yoga: The Psyche Body Connection*, Inner City Books, 2001.

it is part of the body, mind, and soul of the iwi. No doubt, no geneticist could find those genes; they are spiritual. For many centuries, Mt. Taranaki was revered and energized with spiritual practices that flow through its descendants. The mountain is connected to the Earth's fire; it is a living volcano, and that fire can rise and overflow, cleansing the land around it, leaving it more fertile for the years ahead. When the fire is out, the mountain is once again still and serene, its pilgrims starting new paths to its peak.

The mountain is part of the Earth Goddess known to Māori as Papatuanuku. The fire and cone of Mt. Taranaki touch the sky god, Rangi. The mountain is the space between Rangi and Papatuanuku where human life takes place. The mountain occupies a pyramid-shaped space that in abstract looks like a yogi meditator. The mountain connects to the sacred center of the world. Many cultures honor a sacred mountain as well as sacred trees. There are many besides Mt. Taranaki: Mt. Meru in India, the golden mountain at the center of the Earth; Mt. Ararat in Turkey, where Noah's ark is thought by some to rest; Mt. Shasta in northern California, where encounters with intelligent beings from inside the mountain are recorded; Mt. Fuji in Japan, the ancient stairway to heaven and revelation; Olympus in Greece, the home of the gods; and many others.

Mt. Taranaki is the mountain that Chief Paramena would have identified with, the mountain of the Ngāti Tama people. In Te Urewera, where the Tuhoe leader of a redemption movement, Rua McKenna lived, Maungatahapu was the mountain where his New Jerusalem was located, attracting Māori who had had enough of the hard Pākehā world.

Another way of comprehending the Māori relationship between a tribe and a mountain is to call the relationship a synecdoche, in which a part stands for the whole. A familiar use of synecdoche is to say the Crown stands for the Queen or King, in which case, the Crown represents everything that is the royal personage. For Māori, there are natural and prominent landscape features of which the whole tribe is part. In this case, Mount Taranaki can stand for the Te Ati Awa and Ngāti Tama peoples, as well as the other tribes who whakapapa to it.

When I first saw Mount Taranaki two years ago, it was emotionally gripping and spoke to me about why it could lead a people through millennia. Walking in the black volcanic sand on the shore in the city of New Plymouth, beyond which Taranaki is located, I could glance eastward and see the volcano. The land began at sea level where I was standing; when my gaze pivoted from shore to inland mountain, the rising wonder of Mt. Taranaki transfixed me. The volcano was like an alien ship, a blue, shimmering vertical cone planted in otherwise ordinary horizontal land. Each time I looked at it, I expected it to be gone, back to Venus maybe, where they have so many volcanoes they wouldn't have missed this one. The symmetrical cone, standing 2,518 meters above the sea, was a perfect, otherworldly shape for a person like myself from the flat land of Florida.

I could understand why its symmetry has encouraged comparisons with Mt. Fuji in Japan, which was why filmmakers used it in the backdrop for the film, *The Last Samurai*. This was my first view of the unearthly being, and I couldn't stop looking. Taranaki was powerful and the people who claim ancestry from it have something inside that I don't. Perhaps, only during the French revolution, when the term *éruption* and the metaphor of the volcano was widely adopted, did a mountain merge so completely with a group of people.[13] Like a volcano spreading unstoppable fires over the landscape, it was promised that the revolution would spread a purifying fire over the nations, burning to ashes the old establishment and governments. I thought that surely, Paramena would have prayed for the purifying fire of Mt. Taranaki to incinerate the British colonial government—but perhaps that's just the way I would have thought about the situation.

In New Plymouth, where Mount Taranaki dominated the eastern horizon, I found his presence unsettling. I consulted *Lonely Planet*, which exulted climbing him as the second-best thing to do in the world. However, from my view, Mount Taranaki was still angry about quite a few things, so staying off his slopes until the local iwi permitted visitors

---

[13] David Bresson, *Scientific American*, February 19, 2012, online.

was recommended. The British confiscated him in 1885, although his majesty was affronted when, in 1770, Captain Cook named him Mt. Egmont, after John Perceval, the second lord of Egmont. Egmont had encouraged Cook to explore the uncharted lands of the southern seas. Imagine how Taranaki felt to be named after an Englishman who had supported the rout of Aotearoa! When the mountain's Māori name was restored, a journalist tracked down the Earl of Egmont's descendants and asked them how they felt about the change. They immediately described it as a "gross insult" to the family. When the reporter asked if the current Earl had ever visited Taranaki, the reply was no, but he had always wanted to go to Africa.

Although Taranaki has regained his Māori name, I feel his terrible, massively surprising, snow-covered façade is still daunting. When I was there, looking up at the volcano, I felt Taranaki had the power to bless and curse, just like all great taniwha and their descendants. Therefore, I was not surprised to find that, according to local Māori people, Mt. Taranaki is a taniwha, a supernatural being who is powerful and unpredictable. In 2017, the iwi who protect it signed a joint agreement with the government that will see the mountain become a legal personality, like the Whanganui River and Te Urewera.

It is too facile to say that Chief Paramena would have been happy to see the return of Taranaki, the sacred mountain, to his people. He might simply say, "It's home." I remembered that after visiting his daughter Rangi's grave, he had said to me in divination, "Something departs, and something arrives." The mountain had gone to the British like a prisoner, and now had come back to its descendants.

Today, we have almost no Māori people in my county. By traveling to the North Island, where there are many Māori people, I've come to know Aotearoa in a fresh way. Māori has regained status as an official language, and it is the new cool to speak it. Even the *New York Times* has taken notice. The ancient wananga, which were schools for esoteric knowledge where specialists were trained, are resurrected today in public wananga on contemporary campuses, where Māori teach Māori traditional and new technological skills. Te Wānanga o Aotearoa is the country's second largest tertiary education provider, and last year, this school provided training and education to almost 32,000 students. I think almost anyone from Paramena's day would be surprised, because the Māori was supposed to be a dying people. Far from dying, the Māori nation has rebirthed its aesthetics and values and emerged from the dominating white colonial culture. Māori designs are sought after and Māori artists and writers are cutting edge.

Because of this transformation in the Māori estate since Paramena's life ended here, I look back on Wainui's past with the attitude that "The past is a foreign country; they did things differently there." For instance, in 2018, there was a celebration at the new ocean gate leading to Abel Tasman Park. By then, even I, a white Miamian turned Kiwi, knew some te reo. I could understand a lot of what the kaumatua from our county chanted and prayed, his words filled with the awe of nature. I deeply felt the connection he created, and the birds of the forest responded with a brilliant morning chorus as the dawn broke. I haven't heard its intensity repeated since. After this moving ceremony, the mana whenua invited everyone for breakfast at the marae, and the Pākehā competed for knowledge among themselves of Māori language and culture. The last chief of Wainui had to speak English; Māori was outlawed. In 2018, not only were we Pākehā singing in Māori, we were singing joyously.

Somehow, in the world of the Māori, answers appear for me and signs are posted when I need them. For instance, the intriguing manifestation of the impenetrable door of light John and I experienced on the first night we were in Aotearoa, had occurred on a hill near Rotorua, where many Māori people still live. Only in 2019 did I discover more about this light, when I happened to meet the wisdom keeper of Māori artefacts in the Museum of Opotiki, in the Bay of Plenty.

The hill my husband and I walked on that first night of arrival was on the shore of Lake Okataina in the Rotorua area. We revisited the lake and path in 2019 on the first part of our North Island journey, but the lake and path were very still as if sleeping. I hadn't realized that a volcano, Mt. Tarawera stands nearby the lake, a short distance on a map.

I discovered from the lake's lodge owner, that the most recent eruption of Mt. Tarawera occurred in the early hours of the tenth of June, 1886. The eruption lasted six hours and caused massive destruction. It destroyed several villages, along with the famous silica hot springs known as the Pink and White Terraces. It was the deadliest eruption in New Zealand since the arrival of Europeans. Up to one hundred and fifty people, mostly Māori, were killed, and many settlements were destroyed or buried. A member of the Whakatohea iwi told us that the lake and its residents were covered in ash; those who didn't escape all died. Soon after, neighbouring iwi gathered to give land to the survivors.

I told the wisdom keeper about our experience on the path, and she said she could relate something important that had happened since that time, three decades ago, when we were there. She described a prayer ceremony that had been held in 2016 on the hill by the lake, close to where, in 1980, we had come to a standstill in front of the door of light. The prayer ceremony had addressed the spirit of a rangatira, who had been seen wearing a cloak and standing on the same path. He was recognized as a chief of the people long gone, scattered by the eruption of Tarawera. His apparition frightened visiting school children and their teachers. They related the sighting to others, who subsequently arranged for the ceremony to help the chief's spirit move on. Since the ceremony, there have been no more sightings or stories like ours. It was odd, but the wisdom keeper, who is eight-four years old, looked like Aroha's mother Netta.

5. TANIWHA RISING

*I saw a taniwha
when swimming in the Waikato.
He whispered sweetly in my taringa,
"Won't you come along with me?
There's such a lot to see
underneath the deep blue sea.*

— Children's song

*The highest good is like water.
Water benefits ten thousand beings,
Yet it does not contend.
Nothing under heaven is as soft and yielding as water.
Yet in attacking the firm and strong,
Nothing is better than water.*[14]

— Tao Te Ching

A‍ROHA ROPATA WILL ALWAYS BE tangata whenua here in Wainui. The harakeke pa,[15] the palms, and fruit trees she planted, still define the section of land where she lived. Every time I walk there, I think of her, along with the peaceful people and their weavings, songs and gardens. As well as her weaving, I remember Aroha's karanga, as she called out to the directions, in front of her old glass house, gone now.

---

[14] Alfred Huang, trans. *The Complete I Ching*, Inner Traditions, Vermont, 1998, p.54.
[15] A cultivation of several species of flax for weaving and other uses.

I conjure her presence with the black and white photos I made of her the night before she left to study Māori. In these photos she has a large conch which she is using to accompany her karanga.

Aroha's mother, Netta, who visited Wainui many times, is also tangata whenua. On the millennium, Netta sat patiently for hours in a café in our village, where I had an exhibition of drawings and paintings. She talked to all who came, sitting straight and tall, with a dignified presence, comfortable and at home. Sitting with her was a Māori woman everyone called Auntie or Whaea, who blessed the works, Aroha and me. The exhibition, *Evolution*, documented Aroha's transformation from Alison to Aroha, when she discarded her Pākehā identity and took up the name and identity Netta had bestowed on her at birth.

Aroha performing a karanga to the four directions

Netta died many years ago, but at the near culmination of her life, she was present when Aroha graduated in Māori Studies, having learned the language of her mother's birth. She is now one of our ancestors on the Wainui River. Netta is part of our river and land in Wainui; I think she is a taniwha who can be honoured at the sacred pool. Great people become taniwha after death.

Netta was tempered by fire. After her parents' accidental deaths, she and her ten siblings were placed in an orphanage in Nelson, where they were cruelly treated by the Catholic nuns. Netta's language was taken away, and she was forced not only to speak English, but also to be a maid to the nuns and the white orphans. The other Māori girls had to work as maids to the white orphans, too. This was the "job" the nuns said they were preparing the Māori girls to apply for when they left the orphanage. The nuns also told Netta and her sisters, Māori girls' feet were "too big", so Netta and her sisters were given used shoes that were sizes smaller in length and width than their feet. The sisters had to sleep on the floor of a cold corridor outside the white children's rooms. Nelson is freezing in the winter, and there was no heating in the corridor. Netta's younger sister coughed constantly, bleeding more and more frequently into her pillow at night. The nuns taunted her in front of others, saying that Māori women were dirty because they bled from the mouth. Before Netta's little sister died of tuberculosis, she was forced to wash her bloody pillowcases in the icy water outside.

During all this, Netta survived, caring for her brothers and remaining sisters as best she could, walking every morning before dawn to see her younger brothers in their boys' orphanage, helping them dress, and reminding the boys of who they really were, who their parents were, and speaking positively about their Māori culture. I attended her funeral where I met her brothers for the first time. I heard them praising Netta's strength and endurance, and how her love in the mornings, when she walked to them through frost and darkness, kept them alive. These were big men who had also lived through the times of racist degradation and Māori resistance. They looked back on Netta as their salvation, recalling her with gentle words that praised her generous spirit.

What Netta suffered at the hands of the British Catholics was not unique to the orphanage. Born in the 1920s, she grew up in the aftermath of the colonial conquest, so never knew a world where her people were intact or empowered. Netta's grandfather, Papi Ropata, was blackbirded by whalers from Tahiti. After ten years of slavery to the whalers, he managed to jump ship in New Zealand, where he married Aroha's grandmother. She was one of the Ngāti Māmoe, who had subsumed the earlier Waitaha peoples. Aroha's whānau had their own history of oppression, not unlike Ernie's Lucumí ancestors who were kidnapped by slavers in West Africa. Few people know there was a slave trade, forced labor, and terrible racist brutality in the Pacific, too, such as Papi Ropata endured. Netta was a slave to the Catholic nuns and many Māori helped to build and clean the Pakeha world. Aroha has searched twenty years for her ancestral home in the Pacific, away from Aotearoa, and now lives in French Polynesia, where she cultivates land, fishes, and guides tourists on snorkeling trips. She is within a few hours of one of the most sacred sites in the Pacific, Taputapuatea,[16] where she often goes to meditate and talk to her ancestors.

It was Aroha who first told me that the Wainui River and its falls are touched by spirit. There is great mystery around the river, falls and forest. When people arrive in Wainui, they are part of the ordinary, everyday world. Then, when they walk up the river to the falls, they enter a separate reality, one where there can be reverence, peace and deep spiritual connection if the visitor is patient and focussed. This link between place and spirit is aided by the Wainui taniwha, Ngarara Huarau, an archetypal mythic creature who existed in the wild that once was. According to Wainui legend, the local taniwha, Ngarara Huarau, sometimes materialised as a large reptile, frightening villagers. Earlier

---

[16] Taputapuatea is a large marae complex at Opoa in Taputapuatea, on the south eastern coast of Raiatea. The site features a number of marae and other stone structures, and was once considered the central temple and religious center of Eastern Polynesia. In 2017, the Taputapuatea area was inscribed on the UNESCO World Heritage Sites list, with Taputapuatea Marae described as the heart of the site.

Māori people were very respectful of him. Author Philip Simpson speculates that a large native reserve, created in 1847 around our coastline, would have represented land of great value to the Māori, possibly protecting the taniwha.[17]

The Wainui legend said that Ngarara Huarau lived in a cave by the ocean, where he guarded the entrance vigilantly. Ngarara Huarau attacked people who walked by and, some say, ate them. Warriors tried to kill him, but he proved unstoppable. Then, one day, an alluring young woman walked by, beguiling the taniwha with her charm and beauty. He relaxed with her, and they seemed to get along well. Eventually, she invited him to her village just over the mountain. The besotted and trusting taniwha agreed to visit and meet her relatives, who, unknown to the taniwha, were planning his demise. When he arrived, they greeted him kindly, feasting him with local delicacies. Fully sated, he slept. When they were certain he was deeply asleep, the locals surrounded the house where he slumbered and set it aflame. Screams were heard from the house, which was completely immolated.

Some say Ngarara Huarau escaped, mortally wounded, racing to get to his home in the Wainui waters, trailing blazes of fire. There he raged through the uplands, making deep caverns and caves in the limestone. Finally, to end his misery, he dove into the upland Wainui River, deep in thick, ancient forest. The swiftly moving current carried him down the river, where he plummeted over the waterfall, digging a deep pool below, his huge scales falling off and turning to rocks, before continuing his winding journey to the sea. If you stand on the swing bridge on the track, you can look down the river and see the winding path of Ngarara Huarau. Upriver, his tail perpetually plummets down the high, cascading waters of the falls.

When the river is in flood and turning reddish brown from rotting upland vegetation, it is said the taniwha is bleeding and dying again. I'm told by local people, this is the time to pray to him. I see a few similari-

---

[17] Philip Simpson, *Down the Bay, A Natural and Cultural History of Abel Tasman National Park*, Potton and Burton, Nelson, 2018, p.22.

ties between Ngarara Huarau and other rising god myths throughout the world. These were gods like Osiris, Attis and Dumuzi, who died and were dismembered, then reconstituted their life force to regenerate human spiritual life and align with natural laws. These gods each had a woman who set off their powers of regeneration. In the case of Ngarara Huarau, it was Ruru, the maiden, who lured him to her village, where fire transformed him into an immortal. Now the taniwha spirit of Ngarara Huarau is in the falls, in the landslides around the hills, and in the Wainui rain and flood that comes regularly, washing away the illusion of human domination over nature. When the taniwha is in raging flood, the waters stir our subconscious images of a wild uncontrolled Earth. After all, we have had over fifty thousand generations as gatherers and hunters, five hundred as agriculturalists, but only one generation as screen junkies in a post-industrial world. Our fears are ancient, like our beliefs. The stories of taniwha introduce an element of danger to the stability of the Earth that we take for granted.

When I saw the Oscar-winning film, *The Shape of Water*, I was fascinated by the water-man, an amphibian taniwha of many powers, and I thought of Ngarara. A brilliant film, it captures the nature of an amphibious creature, part of a lost, ancestral world. In the creature's water world, simple human virtues of compassion, love and cooperation had the greatest survival value. The water-man, who was captured in the Amazon River, had powers both to heal and harm. However, the military desired these power. The only way to have them, they decided, was to dissect him, but first they would conduct "tests". In the film, the water-man never exercised his true strength until tortured and taxed beyond tolerance. A young, mute woman helped him escape from gunfire into the dark ocean waters near the military testing laboratory. The two of them embraced deeply under water, the mute woman unconscious from a gunshot wound. We watched the water-man restore her life; the woman appeared to have four gill-like marks on her neck. In the end, the vast ocean swallowed them, and we creatures of the land, were left behind.

The Shape of Water gave me another idea about Ngarara. Ngarara had loved Ruru. He was capable of the deep love that allows you to sacrifice yourself to love another. He must have known the villagers would attack him for his love of their kinswoman. Ngarara was capable of trust, too, when he agreed to visit and stay with his lover. And who knows, maybe Ruru really loved him? When I thought of him this way, he seemed more of a man and less of a monster. He had extreme sides; like the river he became, he could be both enchantingly attractive or tumultuously destructive.

When I think about it, water is a shape-shifter, changing around us without our control, holding us in a life-and-death grip from which there is no escape. We not only need water, we *are* water. We hardly think of it unless we have to buy it, but we walk on it when it's solid, paddle and sail on it when its liquid, inhale its components when its gaseous. We cleanse with it, cook with it, drink it, grow every single thing we eat with it, heal ourselves with it, and keep ourselves alive by ingesting it. When water is withdrawn from the world, everything withers and dies. Few of us recognise the preponderant role water plays on our cherished planet. Water is our life, always moving, never still, travelling from one state to the next. The transforming shapes of water, through precipitation, evaporation, freezing, melting and condensation, are all part of the hydrological cycle—a never-ending global process of water circulation from clouds to land, to the ocean, and back to clouds.

This cycling of water is intimately linked with energy exchanges among the atmosphere, ocean and land. These exchanges determine the Earth's climate and cause much of its natural climate variability. According to NASA, the impacts of climate change on the quality of human life occur primarily through changes in the water cycle. I think of the taniwha moving with all the water of the Earth, across time and space, in rain and clouds and sea and river. In Māori stories, the taniwha is intimately connected to changes in the water cycle and enormous landscape catastrophes like the creation of the Wainui Falls and the giant sinkholes in the Pikikirunga/Canaan Downs.

The Gaia hypothesis proposes that all organisms and their inorganic surroundings on Earth are closely integrated in a single, self-regulating, complex system, which maintains the conditions for life on the Earth, with water a large part of this. I find this hypothesis more enlightening for my understanding of life than wave-particle duality, or more recent string theory, although the idea of parallel universes in a multiverse is appealing. In fact, physicists are now debating, in sometimes amusing ways on YouTube, why there is something in our universe when, according to their theories, there ought to be nothing.

"We forget that nature itself is one vast miracle transcending the reality of night and nothingness. We forget that each one of us in his personal life repeats that miracle," wrote the great philosopher of science and natural history, anthropologist Loren Eiseley.[18]

For me, the taniwha is an elemental property in the water, comprised of many spiritual elements taking part in the balance of Gaia, a portion of the vast miracle that is always working to transcend nothingness.

That question posed by our greatest scientific minds, who think there ought to be nothing in the universe, makes me smile as I look over the forest around me, the birds flying by me, the weka babies, big black fluff balls but tough, chasing sparrows across the lawn. I must bring myself back. Nature is absorbing, beautiful and whole. It cannot be compared to social media or anything on a screen. There is no equation that can represent a single part of it. Simply walking down my drive, I am challenged to see everything, the new algae, the nests that have fallen, the mysterious wind that only moves a few cabbage tree leaves. When the big collider in Cern isn't available for experimentation, the ever-evolving natural world offers opportunities for enlightenment whenever I choose. I return to my own experience of veriditas, that elusive sacred something, everlastingly in motion. Veriditas is something, but I can't say what. Wild waters reverberate with this sacred trill attracting us to them to renew ourselves.

Masaru Emoto was a Japanese author and entrepreneur who demonstrated that human consciousness has an effect on the molec-

---

[18] Loren Eiseley, *The Firmament of Time*, originally published by Atheneum in 1960, reprinted by Library of America, 2016.

ular structure of water. Emoto showed us, through jewel-like photos, the reaction of water to words as opposite as hate and love. Two water samples, which had the words hate and love spoken with emotion over them, were quickly frozen so they might be photographed. They showed what you might expect: hate is disorganized chaos, cracked and jagged; love radiates harmonically in a pattern of great beauty. The late Dr. Emoto's technique is more complex than I have described, and his photographs more intriguing. However, the idea of emotions affecting water has caught on, and people meditate to heal water in ceremonies all over the world. I guess the lesson might be: don't disrespect water or forget that it is a sacred gift. Our own virtue or vice affects it strongly, suggesting a feedback loop between the water cycle and us. We are one with our water and with the taniwha.

Respect for the taniwha flows from the statement quoted earlier by NASA, which says, "the impacts of climate change and variability on the quality of human life occur primarily through changes in the water cycle." Certainly, climate change causes more large storms and floods, big winds and heavy weather. Homo sapiens has removed precious habitat, reduced species numbers by fifty percent, and literally excreted where it eats, a dangerous practice where water is concerned. All of this may be angering the taniwha spirit in the water. I've decided it's a good idea not to incite a taniwha, and to offer to taniwha whatever fruits of the water are most appropriate. But it's more important to plant trees around rivers, lakes, waterways, drains and seasides. The banks support life and are necessary for the purity of the water. Only pure water can support adequate amphibious life, the small life under rocks and in the sand on riverbanks and on the ocean's shores.

I like to speculate about mythological stories like Ngarara's and link them to my own lived experiences. I picture the destructive side of the taniwha as veriditas writ large and dangerous, living as elemental energies inside volcanoes or earthquakes, giant storms and flash floods, the side of Ngarara Huarau that wreaked catastrophe in the land and water. Overall, I picture the taniwha as the sum of the energy moving through the water cycle—flood, heavy rain, mud slides, giant waves and strong currents—which can flash through in earthquake destruction or tsunami apocalypse and change us forever. I've felt the power of the taniwha in the typhoon and hurricane many times, but the most memorable time was in Micronesia.

When we met the taniwha, we were snorkeling with mask and fins in the ocean at the uninhabited end of the island of Kosrae, looking at a reef with many varieties of tropical fish. The weather was calm and sunny, the water almost body temperature. Without any warning, no rain or clouds, the sound of a BIG freight train came down the mountainside above the waters where we were snorkelling. This train roar reverberated around us, accompanied by pounding rain, while a higher wind created a big swell which broke over us every few seconds. Everything turned grey, when only minutes before the tropical Sun had blasted us. We floated and waited, while washed over by waves created by the swell, repeatedly blowing water out our snorkels. Arms joined, kicking strongly in the direction of land, for ten minutes we saw nothing in the absolute white-out. Suddenly, to our astonished relief, everything quietened. The noise, rain and wind abruptly quelled, then, within two minutes, disappeared completely. Before we could swim a hundred meters, it was like nothing had happened.

"What was that?" we asked one another when we reached shore. We removed our gear, still stunned by the unique and forceful event which had vanished as quickly as it had appeared. We made our way across the rutted track to the village of our friend, Salek, which was adjacent to the forest and the reefs.

Salek has lived on Kosrae all his life, and fishes regularly from his dugout. He is also the guardian of the most ancient ruins on the island, the temple of the breadfruit goddess, Sinlaku.

"A new typhoon came down the mountaintop this morning," Salek said, "It will strike China soon. This is where typhoons that strike China are born."

After chatting with Salek, we returned to the other end of the island, where we had a small room with intermittent internet. Already, there were warnings about a typhoon in the western Pacific. Within two days, it struck China, a category 4 storm that caused immense damage. I could believe the "thing" that came down the mountain was a monster in any language, a dangerous taniwha. During such an event, if I were an indigenous person seeking a way to describe what I had experienced, and convey it to others over time, I might describe this terrifying force as a rushing dragon, flying down the mountain, roaring toward the East, spewing danger from its mouth, bringing unexpected chaos to a formerly orderly world. When this dragon flew over us, I had been congratulating myself for finding such a remote spot where we could swim alone from the shore to the reef. The power of the taniwha dragon humbled me, reducing me to my flimsy, vulnerable self, swimming in deep waters, wondering what next and hanging on for life. Perhaps that is what all of us are doing, wherever we are at this time: hanging on for life.

6. THE PATTERN IN THE WATER

The spiral in a snail's shell is the same mathematically as the spiral in the Milky Way galaxy, and it's also the same mathematically as the spirals in our DNA.

— Joseph Gordon-Levitt

ACCORDING TO YOGIC PHILOSOPHY, I was born with a karmic inheritance of mental and emotional patterns—known as samskaras—through which I cycle over and over again during my life. Samskaras are my conditioning, which locks me in habitual patterns, predictable and unconscious. "The ruts of the mind," I call them. Before I learned about samskaras, I didn't have a visual picture of why habits are so difficult to challenge. Ruts come in every size from manifest habits like drinking coffee in the morning to unconscious beliefs I have that certain things are imaginary and others are real, and that I am among the few who know the difference.

For instance, taniwha might be dismissed out of hand as an historic and fanciful account of imaginary monsters, if I allow my familiar mental highways to guide me. But if I stay open, I find new concepts and ideas that enhance my enjoyment of the world. I have seen streets called Ngarara Huarau in several towns on Te Ika a Māui. Were there sightings of the water-man on these streets at one time? The taniwha of our local story, who was described as a mean, ugly lizard, may have been a dinosaur relative, an ancient Jurassic beast who survived by hiding in the rugged landscape. Or he may have been more.

I am reading *The Matriarch* by Witi Ihimaera, who describes the gorgeous, brilliant matriarch who wears glistening pearls in her hair, as a taniwha, half human, half supernatural. She is brilliant and beautiful; she is the kuia who controls her whānau with commanding charisma. The assembled chiefs are in awe of her vast ancestral knowledge. To call her a taniwha is to acknowledge all her rare capabilities.

The taniwha is a compelling metaphysical and mythic figure who helps people draw the supernatural close. Taniwhas connect people with their ancestors, like Maui, the culture hero of Polynesia, who caught the North Island using a fish hook made from his grandma's jaw, and who become a taniwha after he died. The gods are half mortal, and they speak from the fifth dimension. We all know the first three dimensions, length, width and depth; the fourth is time, or position in time; and the fifth is a transcendent view of the first four. Great beings, a taniwha like Maui, view human life from this dimension, although who knows how many dimensions they actually occupy since they can act as gods and men.[19]

I kept thinking there was something more that I could understand near the river, something about Ngarara Huarau. I wasn't of Māori descent. I had no iwi or ancestral stories. My feeling came from proximity and absorption of the spirit of place over time. There was an equinox coming, and I decided to hold a small observance on the river. Ceremony sets aside a time outside normal daily life, and I'm always pleased how quickly ceremonies conjure a holiday mood over me. I think it's because I remember a time when we were all free to communicate with nature and spirit on our own, no church or mosque necessary. For me, ceremony is a time to plunge into mystery, supplication, and to be heartrendingly grateful to the incredible planet we live on. It is also a time for blessings to flow back. It can be private or secret or public, it doesn't matter; ceremonial action is healing to me, you, everything. It

---

[19] There are, of course, many dimensions in our multiverse, and most cultures have far more than five spiritual dimensions and domains. All indigenous cultures consider different kinds of entities dwell in these different planes, which are contacted by shamans and mediums.

calls in the fifth dimension, and for a time I see a more commanding perspective, which melts away my unsettled mind, leaving me soft and reborn.

The Lucumi believe that that everything in the universe has its own destiny. Just as I do, the taniwha and the spiny weta have their own destinies and souls. How did this astonishing set-up on Earth happen, where we are embedded in the evolving landscape, related to the whole? Did it start with a single organism at the bottom of the seas, which mutated when volcanoes exploded or when comets hit the Earth? What about the green forests and the blooms in spring? Clear water in the flowing river running over rocks that shine with gold and silver? A Sun that is our life, just right for us, and our food? Earth is a superlative twenty-jillion-star restaurant where we eat our delicious way through our days. In my diet, and in my breath, I have absorbed nearly everything Earth has to offer. These have become part of me, part of everything. Ceremony stops the world of time and caresses the eternal *now*. It stimulates reflection and play.

As an example, I'll describe a ceremony I carried out on Ernie's advice. Two years ago, Ernie had divined that an important personal cycle for me would end and another begin on a specific day in September. Coincidentally (as I discovered after his reading), the date he recommended was the day of the fall equinox, a total solar eclipse, and a new moon; the day after this would be an international celebration for World Water Day. It was an astrologically power-packed time. I decided my ceremony would take place at the sacred pool on the river, where I go to pray to the ancestral spirits of place. The synchronous cosmic and planetary movements that day meant my hours on the river would be supercharged. I made my ritual center an old, grey-barked rain forest tree, which leaned over the river, roots anchored in the golden sand. I enchanted my tree with twinkling yellow candle lights, placed where the swollen roots joined the trunk. Then I danced, sang, and talked sincerely to the tree-being, and to the spirits of the riverbank and river.

I didn't know exactly how to proceed, because two weeks before the ceremony a voice in my head said, "The day you hold your festival, ensure a dog is on the riverbank. It doesn't matter if other people are there."

I thought about those words a long time, and eventually, I decided they felt right. I didn't have a dog, so what dog could I invite to the river for the seasonal observance? After contemplation, I phoned a friend and asked her to bring her puppy. She couldn't come, but she said we could borrow her young dog.

At midday, my husband arrived with an eight-month-old, black and white border collie, Maki. I saw him arrive, sitting on the seat beside John, and when he saw me, he started to bark. I opened the back hatch and spoke a greeting to a wriggling puppy, soft as silk and happy to be having an adventure. Then, to my enormous surprise, he stopped barking and jumped out of the back of the car. Maki ran to the trees by the river, and when he reached the riverbank, immediately trotted across the granite riverbank stones and leapt into the cold, clear water.

White foam, on top of the black river water, had been shaped by current into a wide, turning spiral at the center of the pool. The puppy swam into the surface of this helix, leaving a trail through the froth. He swam through opaque bubbly foam toward a small stick my husband had thrown. Maki reached the swirling stick, carried it back to shore, and dropped it at John's feet. He then turned around and sat on his haunches in the water, looking across the pool to the centre of the spiralling current.

Forty times, or more, my husband tossed the stick to the center of the river. Each time, the puppy swam easily upstream in the swirling water, even putting his head under. Not once did he leave the water; rather he sat shaking, thigh deep in the cold shallows, concentrating his gaze on the center of the pool, waiting to make another leap. After a half hour, the dripping pooch came out of the river with hardly a glance to us, shook himself vigorously, and walked up the sand path to higher ground.

The whole display had been Maki's idea. I'd not planned what role he would play in my ceremony. In fact, listening to that voice in my head, and fetching the dog on the day, was all I had needed to do. The sounds of Maki's leaping and splashing had been like a swimming pool filled with children playing water games, just the right ambiance for a river fete on the equinox, almost World Water Day, new moon, and total solar eclipse. The fact that it was completely spontaneous made it all that much lighter. We had laughed and shouted and danced around in the shallows, during which time my outlook changed dramatically. I had thought magic gone from the sacred pool. Instead, it was the best ceremony possible for the day, the water, the Moon, the Earth and the Sun.

Later, the puppy's owner said that her pup had done nothing like this before. During his long swim, the small collie drew my attention again and again to the coiling vortices of froth in the dark river. I imagined the taniwha had taken temporary possession of Maki; the mythical being was attracted by the puppy's youth and enthusiasm, and by my intention to honour the important day at the sacred waters on the river. I once read that taniwha were sometimes linked with the early, magical and fabled Māori dogs called kuri. For that reason, I was attracted to the idea that Maki had revealed the taniwha writing on the river's surface. W. B. Yeats, in *The Second Coming,* describes it:

> Turning and turning in the widening gyre
> The falcon cannot hear the falconer.

The small black and white dog was in this falcon state, swimming in widening liquid circles, tuned in to something I couldn't hear, yet aware of the deeper taniwha force. Nature used Maki as a vehicle to reveal the taniwha, even suggesting to me, through an inner voice, that I bring Maki on the day of the ceremony. Taniwha are powerful spirits of place, and during my observances on the river, I experienced more than a strictly symbolic encounter with these wild, natural powers. The life in the river manifested physically in the young dog's swimming spirals, just as it did in the curving dragon's path the taniwha described on its way from the waterfall to the sacred pool.

In its most universal meaning, the spiral shows the integration of human consciousness with nature, representing the journey which life follows to the center and out again. Beginning at least in the Neolithic, ancient cultures all over the world painted spiral designs on rock walls and caves; eventually, there were labyrinths, spiral dances and spiral stairways. Many of us have seen spirals carved on megalithic structures in the British Isles and Europe. Spirals are seen in a diverse range of organic phenomena like sea shells, galaxies, cabbages and water going down a drain. Spirals may symbolise nature expanding outward from a source, the center and the ever-evolving, curving arm that comes back on itself and goes forward many times. A spiral might be seen as a water symbol; obviously, the river pool was inscribed with one, and Maki followed its course and speed, while the water was rippling in circles. So, Maki had something to show me, the signature of Ngarara Huarau in the river pool.

If I desire to be guided by the spirit of nature, or to talk to an ancestor at a special spot of beauty or mana, like the sacred pool, I say aloud, "Thank you, I love you, I'm sorry, please forgive me". This is an Ho'oponopono practice from Hawaii that I find deeply effective. It is practised by Hawaiian shamanic healers. The words release a lot of feeling for me. I prayed these phrases in Wainui and to its forest, waters and taniwha, and I also apologised to the land and water for the actions of my own ancestors. Although my ancestors never asked my permission, they too cut down a native forest and established a dairy farm on formerly indigenous land during the American holocaust of Indians. The period of native extinction from 1880-1920 in Pennsylvania, when diseases and settler land grabs removed Indians from the state, was the same time colonisation forces in New Zealand removed Māori from the lowlands of Aotearoa, where they had lived for centuries. My own ancestors profited a great deal from this in Pennsylvania. Not only did they receive a land grant, they cut the forest to plant crops and graze dairy cows, and they extirpated all the fur-bearing animals. With the removal of forest and animals, the Indians had no living left, and their land was taken for settlement. The correspondence between the two colonial invasions is striking. In Aotearoa, Paramena even had to pay to buy back Crown land that his iwi had collective ownership of before the surveyors and settlers came. The Māori had no living left, just like the Pennsylvania Indians.

I know there is a chain of human terror and violence stretching for thousands of years through many civilizations. Pennsylvania and New Zealand are not exceptions. The pacific periods seem exceptional. The empires, kingdoms, states, religions, popes and priests, bureaucrats and businesses find ways to oppress common enemies and control resources. I don't want to belabour this point, because we all have one understanding or another of how we got to this situation, where our environment is threatened by us, overwhelmingly so it appears. There is a lot of grief in this veracity for each of us; we hold it in our hearts collectively.

If I speak the Ho'oponopono words to a tree, the river, the sky or the ocean, a deep sorrow about what we have done to nature pours out of me; and at the conclusion, I am much lighter—so much so, sometimes, I can't remember my troubles. In any case, I repeat the phrases until I feel the soul of the words: *I love you. I'm sorry. Please forgive me. Thank you.* When I become fully conscious of the apocalypse my species has wrought on the Earth, the *I'm sorry* feels received by the plants. They shake me deeply, empty me, and fill me with joy.

Destiny is, in many ways, my most important spirit guide, but my greatest teacher is nature.

7. ALONE WITH THE TREES

We call it the gum tree, as if it were just a thing ...
Not watching, not listening, not stretching, not changing colour,
Not bleeding, not blooming, not breeding, not singing, not shrieking,
Not crying, not sleeping, not grieving.
— From *Gum Tree*, a poem by Graham Ballard

I HAVE READ STORIES OF MYSTICS who received enlightenment from trees. Their tales involve great suffering, including being buried for years under the earth up to their heads, hanging upside down for a lifetime, or sitting stock still in vipassana meditation under the spreading arms of a bodhi tree for at least weeks, probably years, as the Buddha apparently did. I am impressed by these stories and by what the trees transmitted to the seekers of knowledge. I admire those who say, "Yes, let me do whatever it takes to seek the knowledge of trees," and who cultivate ascetic habits and seek disciplined spiritual training that may deliver their wish. I'm not saying I haven't done some of that, but for the moment I call myself a decadent yogi and an accidental shaman. Trees are a big part of my happiness. I often think enlightenment is rated too high and happiness too low; but maybe, in respect to love of nature, they are the same.

True shamanic experiences, where you go to the edge and come back with a personal lifetime vision, are rare and usually acquired with drugs, training, exposure, fasting and other ascetic practices. I've carried out some of those practices in the past, with interesting results. Shamanism is about strengthening our connection to, and finding our own unique destinies within, nature. Shamanism includes animal alliances, special songs, and learning the languages of wind and rain, sky and mountain. Shamanic practitioners often use trance states to search for a client's lost soul, or to see the treatment for an illness. Most shaman have undergone ordeals that, when overcome, leave them with new healing and psychic powers.

While I don't seek these experiences consciously, it seems now that every so often I find myself in the midst of something shamanic, not even recognizing how I got there, like the taniwha cyclone in Micronesia that appeared out of nowhere. During an artists' residency, two years ago, I had an experience of nature that touched me deeply in a way not possible to fully describe. Yet there is something left over from that night that will always be inside me. I remember it as *an intimate encounter with a grove of eucalyptus trees.* In the midst of an almost legendary taniwha storm, a monster that came unexpectedly, like the cyclone, the link between trees and the hydrological cycle, among other things, became clear to me. Trees anchor and attract water. Like Homo sapiens, they cannot live without it. When the trees are gone, the water usually disappears. When you are with trees, you are with water; trees lower and raise their limbs a few inches in cycles each night as they pump water and fluids up to their canopies and down into their roots, which are densely connected to other roots. Trees of the same species make friends and strengthen one another. These facts remind me of the eucalyptus trees.

The artist's residency was located in a planted forest of eucalyptus trees, consisting of several species. Our brief was to make art from the natural materials readily available in the forest. The residency took place over four days, and we had the option of pitching a tent or driving home at night. A small hut was also available. I decided I would pitch a tent and enjoy the deep dreams I have when I sleep on the earth. I erected my tent in the middle of the mature eucalyptus trees that the park was known for. Their canopies were in the sky high above my head, their trunks so tall I could see through to the estuary unobstructed by limbs and leaves. I felt delighted. *This is a forest of giants, and I am a*

Lilliputian six inches tall. I've seen photos of Europeans riding horses though ancient trees on the North Island, before they were destroyed, and the riders looked similarly tiny. Sometimes, it is necessary to remember these giants were once plentiful. I enjoyed returning to the tent because eucalypts are well known for purification and healing, and I felt safe and protected. All was well. Then, late in the afternoon, it started raining.

By 10 p.m. the rain and wind were exceptional, even for a rainy place. Anywhere I happened to touch on the inside of my tent brought a rivulet of water down the side. My sleeping bag was wet underneath, and water was dripping directly onto my head. By 11p.m. my tent was shaking so hard I thought it would fly apart. I decided to return to my car in the parking lot, which was just through the trees to the east. I reasoned it should be an easy right, then straight ahead. I left everything in the tent, except my rain jacket and torch, and stepped out into the night.

The proverbial bad opening line, *it was a dark and stormy night,* didn't begin to describe how uncanny the forest seemed. I thought I could easily walk through the trees to my car, or to the hut where the other artists were sleeping. I turned on my torch, which reflected back from the wall of rainwater falling around me, but I couldn't see further than the trunks of the nearby trees. Shrouded half in mist, half in shadow, their canopies screamed in the increasingly strong gusts of wind. I considered getting back into my tent, but the cold water around my sleeping bag persuaded me to turn in the direction of the parking lot. I stepped toward a blurry group of trees. However, within a very few metres, I realised I couldn't see anything; it would be better to return to the dripping tent after all, and wait out the storm there.

I turned and took a few steps around a tree, expecting to see my tent, but found only straight-boled trees, mist and drenching rain. I was certain it had been there, but my torch reflected on grey bark next to black space with foggy atmosphere all around. I reluctantly grasped that my tent could lie in any direction. I tried one direction then the other, taking steps between trees, but the little gold tent did not materialize in front of me the way I had been imagining it would. Lightning and thunder then commenced in this small theatre of the forest. The lightning illuminated stands of long straight, deep magenta trunks for a few bright seconds when I was sure I would see my tent. The light was followed by thunder, shaking the world with a slow rumble that started far away, rapidly approaching until it cracked with an explosion over my head and through the forest. My tent never come into view, and the thunder was so loud it left me feeling shaken and vulnerable. I could hear the sea pounding down the estuary inlet, maybe twenty metres from me.

Suddenly, my torch went out, and the wall of drenching water and grey mist were gone. I was alone, and even smaller, as if I had disappeared from the landscape. I then thought I might feel my way, so sank onto my hands and knees. I may have crawled around the same tree again and again, water falling in sheets down the sides of my head and face. Drenched and fallen eucalyptus leaves covered my hands, arms and knees, which I wiped on my small raincoat.

I wished I had brought better rain gear, or put an apple in my pocket, better yet a cell phone. I wished I had checked the batteries on the torch. I wished I had stayed home. These remorseful thoughts continued while I groped around the forest floor. I banged the top of my head directly into a tree; luckily, I wasn't crawling very fast. The wind had picked up with gale force gusts, the huge eucalyptus trees shaking their canopies, striking their branches and raining huge volumes of water on my head. There would be a sheet of rainwater continuously blanketing me, then when the wind picked up, buckets of water from the thick foliage joined the sheet of rain. It was like diving into a swimming pool. I crawled a few paces in another direction. Then I realised I had no idea which way I was going, so I stood up.

I said out loud, hopefully, as if someone could hear and direct me, "I'm returning to my tent now." There was no answer.

I turned blindly around another way. I took a few steps in that direction, bumping into a few younger trees with smaller boles. Of course, no tent was there. I finally realized I was out in the forest at near midnight, in high winds and pouring rainfall, without a working torch, wearing only a thin soaked-through raincoat. At last, I decided to call for help. I yelled in my very biggest voice, which is quite large, but there was no reply. Nothing could compete with the sounds of the wind, the trees and the sea.

I knew then I was on my own. I became aware of the waves pounding the shore and water rushing out the channel, roaring past me not far away. I had hardly noticed the water when I pitched my tent, and now the sound was as dominant as the thunder. The thought of going further and accidently stepping into that cold, dark frothing force stopped me taking another step forward, especially when I realized I was walking through water already, which ran over my boots.

My watch said 11:50 p.m. when I halted my confused progress. Luckily, there were intense flashes of light, which reflected on the giant tree trunks around me. On an intermittent flash, I could see I was standing in front of a very large eucalyptus tree. I put my arms around her and found they were maybe half way around her papery trunk. She was strong, I hoped, and would not succumb to the high winds. It was the safest place, really the only possible place, and I decided to stand by that tree no matter what.

By now, the rain was running down inside my raincoat, which was soaked through to my skin. I had no other clothes on, and my socks were filled with water inside my boots, so every movement was a cold, sloshing weight on my feet. The cold water was running down my head, down my face, down my arms and legs, and if I opened my mouth it ran in there, too. It was early November and about nine degrees celsius; not freezing, thank goodness, but cold enough. I started to shake, becoming uncontrollably cold really fast when I ceased my wandering excursions. The cold penetrated more and more as I discovered there was no warmth in the tree that I embraced.

Finally, I said to myself, *think, do something!* So I made a deal with myself. I decided, I'm going to jog in place every fifteen minutes for five minutes. My rule was I could look at my watch only when I believed fifteen minutes had expired, because I had started to compulsively look at the luminous numbers, disappointed every minute I looked, thinking an hour had passed. Every time the wind gusted and howled, pails of water still dumped down on me from the foliage above, leaving me underwater for a few seconds, shaking my head and turning around to find air.

I started running in place, lifting my knees high and going fast, making time fly I thought, but I checked my watch (on the timer mode) and it impossibly revealed that twenty seconds had passed. I was keenly disheartened. I then tried not to check it, did anyway, but somehow finished that first, fast jog. That meant I would wait for fifteen minutes and do it again. I'd worked hard during the timed running in place and expected conditions to change as I warmed. They did not! I did not! Minutes passed without any appreciable difference in my temperature, so I extended the period of jogging, and when I rested, I squatted and wrapped my arms around my legs, a wet lump feeling sorry for herself folded up at the base of the big, wet tree.

I felt tired and wanted to stop, but my teeth were chattering and my shivering body said *keep going*. After what had felt like six or seven hours, I checked the time for the hundredth time, and the dials read 2 a.m. I continued my jogging, but increased it again to five minutes every ten, still right there under the giant eucalyptus tree, swinging my arms in the air as large rivers of water ran down my sleeves, across my body, and down my legs. Between runs, I continued to sink down to the ground at the bottom of the tree. The lightning and thunder created a bizarre light and sound show. The branches, creaking and groaning as the wind blasted them, reminded me of the eucalypts that had fallen down in the last storm. I briefly wondered if I would escape if a big one came down, but I was too cold to worry about it. I figured I would die of the cold first, which was somehow reassuring.

As the lightning continued, I looked up, blocking rain from my eyes, almost enjoying the sight of the trees around my tree in the misty, golden lightning. But oddly, when there was no thunder and lightning, around the big eucalyptus trees just opposite to me a vague glow remained visible through the mist. It was faint but discernible. I was shaking, but my mood lifted. The foliage between two trees was joined as one, outlined by the dim light, which made them appear as a collegial group of trees, giant Australian beings gathered together in this Aotearoa park, sharing a common destiny with me for the night. Would they have koalas in their branches at home? I kept jogging as I watched the trees, who now felt like company, or bemused observers, and realized there was nothing they could do to relieve my plight. They were remote and full, not needy like me, a weak Homo sapiens who had wandered into their grove, lacking basic preparation. The trees were neither ill-equipped, nor disrespectful of nature.

I kept jogging, but it was still another thousand years before it was finally 3:30 a.m. I said to myself, *a couple more hours at the most, keep it up.* By now my chattering teeth were very hard to put up with, and jogging was getting harder and harder. I made myself think about the warmest place in my body, and when I found one that wasn't completely frozen, like a tiny place on my abdomen, I would pretend that same warmth was spreading over me until I was sweating on a hot day in Miami. Actually, it only worked once. After that my freezing body said, *You've got to be kidding me.* Weak mind. I started freezing again.

Soon after, I addressed the still glowing trees in a formal manner. "Trees, I'm soaked through, and I'm freezing. I can't stop shaking. I need a better coat, an umbrella. I'm an idiot. I left my tent with a small torch and a useless rain jacket, and here I am nearly naked in front of you with nothing to cover my icy body except this soaked plastic jacket. I'm here in this grove by chance, unprepared, but I feel I know you."

I heard my words, which seemed to be absorbed by the mist. Was this the Mist Maiden with those wispy, whirling vapours? Was I enchanted? I was laughing, teeth chattering, and simply gave up trying to control anything. Many dark scenarios played in the far reaches of my mind, but I silenced them. *Two more hours.*

I continued my address to the trees, "Tell me what I need. I bet Heaphy and Brunner (Northwest Nelson explorers and surveyors) came through here led by Kehu."

For some reason, it had come into my head that I could talk with

Kehu, who had proved himself the most reliable, brilliant guide, letting his white explorers sleep in while he trapped birds and eels, made fires, and sang. Heaphy came through Wainui. When I read Heaphy's diary of exploring the South Island's West Coast, I decided Kehu was the man to have on a journey. Leave Heaphy behind, if there was a choice.

"Kehu," I called out, because I thought the guide was nearby. "What were you wearing on your long walks up and down the coast, in the rain and snow, never having any shelter?" I really wanted to know. How did anyone stay warm in this weather?

Across the lightning illuminated haze, I heard a voice.

"We had seal skins, Judith. Seal skins for cloaks. That's what you should have now."

There was a feeling of care and love, but I had no way to get any seal skins, of course.

I was getting colder, but the knowledge that I would be able to see when the Sun came up bolstered me. The glow around the tree grove had started to fade. It was 4:00 a.m., and I knew that by 5:30 there would be sunlight enough to disperse the shadows. The rain slowed to a steady downpour, and the wind speed came down. I still kept to my routine.

Finally, around 5:30 a.m., I saw the trees in the rising sunlight, quiet and dripping as the wind stopped. There was water across the land, and I could just see the white-capped estuary through the forest to the side of the path, which turned out to be not more than a meter from the tree where I'd been standing. The parking lot was just meters away, too, but I couldn't have found it before the Sun came up. I had definitely not noticed the thicket of blackberry the day before, which separated the parking lot from the forest. Weaving around the blackberry, I rushed to my car. Luckily, besides the torch, the only thing I'd taken from my tent at 11 p.m. were my car keys.

The drive home felt anticlimactic, and my mood descended. I was back in ordinary reality, which seemed dull, easy, tame and, well, human. The reality of six hours in the huge storm, under the trees, had been direct, bold and vivid. I had been alive. I had been so alive. That was it: I had felt so alive. Even the mist had been alive, and the wind, rain and trees had vibrancy so high it made the inside of my home feel like a dead world. I sat in a warm bath for about three hours before I could feel my feet and hands, but I wanted the elements back. They were strong and penetrating. I had been weak and cold; but at the same time, I had been exhilarated.

That afternoon, I noticed that I felt cut off and disconnected. During the storm, sharing every element with the trees, sky and earth, I felt deeply related to them. We had shared a strong taniwha experience together. I saw the trees. I heard them, and they, me. I thought I understood what Robin Kimmerer meant when she asked, *What would it feel like to be part of a family that includes kauri and kiwi and weta?* I paraphrase; she used North American flora and fauna in that question. She thought we would be less lonely, more connected, feeling like we belonged, and we would be smarter.[20] I think Dr. Kimmerer is correct. I never felt so related and allied to the trees and the elements as I did the night of the storm. We were one together during those wet, miserable, dark hours that yielded so much light.

Later, in the evening, I searched the internet. I found that Heaphy and Kehu could indeed have had seal skins, a warm and waterproof material. While the seal trade was mostly over by the mid-nineteenth century, Heaphy had seen skins being sold when he went down the West Coast. But whether or not they really did have cloaks, I don't know.

I had a dream some years ago, in Australia, that reminds me of my experience in the rain with the giant eucalyptus trees. In my dream, I felt myself sinking beneath the earth, spread long on my back. Giant rain forest trees, their trunks strong and straight, slowly, yet quickly, grew out of my chest, belly, arms and legs. My chest and rib cage felt full, but very relaxed. An Aboriginal woman appeared. She was

---

[20] Professor Kimmerer is Professor of Environmental and Forest Biology at the State University of New York, and she also has an indigenous background as a member of the Citizen Band Potowatomi. I'm reading her lovely work, *Braiding Sweetgrass: Indigenous Wisdom, Scientific Knowledge and the Teachings of Plants*, Milkweed Editions, Canada, 2013.

barefoot, had short clipped hair, and was wrapped in tapa cloth. Long ropes of coloured beads were draped over her neck and shoulders. The woman stood beside the trees, above me, and yet simultaneously, she signalled to me under the earth.

"Come," she said.

I felt comfort and joy across multiple levels, until all was One. In my dream, my fear of death, of being covered by the Earth, vanished.

8. THE OLDEST TREE ON THE MOUNTAIN

If what a tree or a bush does is lost on you,
You are surely lost. Stand still. The forest knows
Where you are. You must let it find you.
— From *Lost*, a poem by David Wagoner

THE HOURS WHEN THE MIND is absorbed by beauty are the only hours when I feel the absence of ego. Often, when I go to the forest, it is to seek its therapy. I have so many sorrows, guilts, burdens and shortcomings, and I go to tell them to the river and the trees.

It's odd, though. I am seldom able to carry through with more than a few sentences before I notice the beauty in front of me. I'm like a blind person for a few minutes, churning this and that inside. But they're sneaky; the green, the air, the mossy rocks lure me to forget my troubles. My eyes are slowly caught by motion, and, oh look, I smile, there is a whio, one of the newly introduced ducks. Then I see the clematis, blooming white flowers down the trees and rocks above the pool; their reflections in the water are astounding. Within minutes, I forget what I came for, and I feel happier. I betray my own suffering in favour of devouring the forest and water with my eyes.

One of the most memorable dreams I've had was after visiting Ernie in Miami, when he showed me his plants and trees in the garden. He had mangos and paw paws, and a variety of other fruits and tropical nuts. He was also growing Lucumi spiritual and herbal plants, even growing cotton which is used in head rogations, rituals to cleanse the crown chakra. Herbal salves and balms emerged from his new butter-making machine, along with lovely creams for the skin, which he gave me to try. After leaving him that night, I had an interesting dream that confirmed we share a deep rootedness through trees. I talk about my dreams because they are a true guide of souls. I remember landmark dreams like this for a long time.

In the dream, I was driving away from Ernie's house. I turned so I could look back on his home one last time before departing for Aotearoa. To my happy surprise, there was an immense tree, the Mother Tree from the film *Avatar*, where Ernie's house had stood. The tree's immense branches wrapped a fairy tale cottage high above the ground, and I thought, *that's where Ernie lives*. If you liked *Avatar*, you probably know that the colossally lush, fern-covered tree was called the Tree of Souls, which provided their closest connection to Eywa, the guiding force and deity for the planet Pandora and its indigenous people, the Na'vi. The Na'vi believed that Eywa, like Gaia, acted to keep the ecosystem of Pandora in perfect equilibrium. This was expressed through their Home Tree, the point of connection with Eywa. *Avatar* touched a deep vein of environmental grief in its audiences, who loved the Na'vi, hated the US military who destroyed the Tree of Souls, and yearned to live on Pandora where pathways were the branches of trees and homes were inside them. In our hearts, many of us want to live in a garden like the planet Pandora, so my dream was both personal and collective.

Trees are at the center of many spiritual paths. They anchor our natural world to the earth, air and water, no matter what a culture believes about them. But if they don't believe that trees do anchor the elements, let them cut them down and experience the tragedy that ensues. There are so many examples now, some stretching thousands of years into the past, like the cultures of the Middle East who had taken the trees down, including the famed cedars of Lebanon, by the time Egypt's pyramids were built. I've always thought those near treeless lands, now desert, are cursed, and their role in the world as a theatre of conflict and war demonstrates it. American Christians, who strive to visit Israel, see it as the place where Armageddon will begin. When they look at the fundamental tragedy that desert lands represent, in terms of lost biodiversity and reduction of resources, it is easy to see why they think the way they do, even though they may not understand it. When I see the lands in the Middle East, they look to me like Armageddon has already begun, which is another reason I give thanks to the Big Tree (we call this tree, our own Tāne Mahuta) every time I look up the mountain behind my home. The Māori god, Tāne Mahuta, is the creator of humans; he is a great forest tree at the beginning of life on Earth. Today, one of his sons is a two thousand year old kauri tree on Te Ika Maui in Northland, an "attraction" that draws ninety thousand tourists a year. Tāne is fenced off in a small park where nearby kauri trees are dying. Their illness is reflected globally in a loss of habitat, of biodiversity, and a lack of forest protection.

Wainui Tāne Mahuta

Prior to creation, Tāne carried out a Herculean labour on which the entire future depended. Darkness filled the cosmos and precluded evolution of life-forms, which must have light and air. In order to dispel darkness, Tāne had to separate his parents, Ranginui and Papatuanuku, who lay in such a close embrace that not even a tiny crack of light came between them. Many gods had tried to separate them, but only Tāne succeeded. By separating Ranginui (the sky) from Papatuanuku (the Earth), Tāne created Te Ao Marama (the world of light). Then Tāne created all the trees and birds in the forest. Some legends say he created people, too. If you want to blame someone for our troubles, blame Tāne for creating us. But the truth is, we've cut him and his forests down, so how can we complain? Tree spirits are no match for sawmills and chain saws. On the other hand, Obatalá, who is the Lucumi creator of human beings, had a reason for messing up. He got drunk during creation and started creating misfits. Tāne and Obatalá are ancient, the first gods remembered across the land of their births, New Zealand and West Africa.

Trees are powerful links to an unremembered past. For instance, the kahikatea tree is New Zealand's tallest forest tree and once dominated lowland swamps and wetlands. Here in Wainui, there is a small area of kahikatea forest, which is full of birds in spring, the chorus loud within the high upper branches. During summers, these tall trees are covered with red berries which birds love, and which were also a food source for Māori. The colonials, whose plan for settlement depended on destroying the native ecosystem, called the tree "white pine", to point out its qualities as timber. The kahikatea dates from the Jurassic period, when neither birds nor flowering plants had yet evolved. I would dearly love to have seen flying dinosaurs eating the berries and falling asleep in the tree's towering branches. Steven Spielberg's famous film, *Jurassic Park*, filmed in the South Island's Fiordland National Park, has convinced me that I can almost conjure the Jurassic Period. However, a big hornbill, flying between trees in the Solomon Islands, is the closest sound I've heard that might resemble a dinosaur flying into the branches of a kahikatea. It's a big sound, a windmill or a whooshing train starting up and coming down the track, and the dino-bird lands with a thud that shakes the foliage on the top of the rainforest giant.

I mentioned earlier that Ernie had introduced me to rituals and ceremonies involving trees, and that his instructions always stemmed from a divination reading with Dilogún shells. Ernie reads my relationship to the universe around me, finding what I need to do to maintain balance and not fall into misfortune. One day in Miami, I visited Ernie for a general reading, which led to a sacred walk to the biggest tree behind our home in Waitaha. Perhaps it was always with this great tree in mind that I wanted to understand the layers of Wainui, because the Big Tree had seen everything and everyone come and go. He was probably a small tree when the first Māori canoes stopped in Wainui, a volunteer waiting to rise to the light, who was to live for centuries and centuries, escaping axe and fire.

"Obatalá sends you blessings, blessings accompanied by fortune," Ernie said, at last. "However, your fortune isn't complete." He had thrown the shells and taken his time before speaking.

"Is there anything I need to do?"

"Your fortune is dependent for its completion on a remedy, a small adimú (food offering). You need to take this to the oldest tree on the mountain. Your salvation is tied to this tree."

My salvation was tied to it. That was a big deal, definitely. I immediately thought of the tree we call Tāne, or the Big Tree, our own Tāne Mahuta. The Māori Tāne is male, so I think of our tallest tree on the mountain as male also; although the riverbank tree is more female to me, just as I felt the eucalyptus I spent the night with during my artist's retreat was a strong woman. Our forest god here has a large white trunk that rises above the rest of the canopy at least a hundred feet. Looking up from the highway, toward the back of the valley, he appears like a lollypop, a great, green round of vegetation atop a long white stick in the middle of the rain forest park. While I talked about this old tree, I could see Ernie paying close attention.

"How old is that tree?"

"He's about eight hundred years old."

"Eight is the number of Obatalá." Obatalá is the creator of humans and the Earth, like Tāne.

I told him about the Big Tree's long, white bole, which stands straight up out of the forest. When you see him that way, you think this tree is the ultimate magic wand, set upright in the middle of the back of the valley, receiving pure vitality and transmitting it around the forest in the national park. Less than two hundred years ago, Wainui was home to thousands of big trees like this one. Unfortunately, perhaps only four others escaped the fires and saws, and still tower above the young canopy, with Tāne the tallest.

Ernie added that Obatalá's colour was white, and he was known as the King of the Earth and the Progenitor of Human Beings—very similar to Tāne. It was like a personal message to us from the nature spirits. "We are all one," they said.

Soon after this reading, I returned to Waitaha and set out in the forest behind my home to visit Tāne with my adimú, the offering Ernie had prescribed. When I entered the forest, a plump robin with grey wings and a mauve-black head greeted me. I saw it to my left in the trees, jumping from branch to branch. It looked at me with intense dark eyes, turning its head from side to side. In two decades, I had only seen a native robin in this forest twice. After a few strides, the gentle uphill path entered a tunnel of fern trees. Looking up, I saw blue sky silhouetting fronds long, dark, and trembling slightly in the gentle breeze. I heard water in the distance, then smelled fresh earth as I descended to a creek running high following a week of rain.

After crossing the fast-flowing creek, the track led me up a steep wall into the forest beyond our land. Suddenly, I was in dense ferns and palms, stepping over creepers tangled across the ground. I extricated myself from some gnarly vine and, as I looked up, beheld a gateway that led to the rain forest in the higher reaches beyond. This portal's side posts were an impressively tall, thick pukatea tree and, a few feet away from it, a tall nikau palm. The two had spanned an arch between them, created by their intertwined fronds and branches. I had never noticed it before, but there it was, a perfectly formed archway. At second glance,

I could see a circle in front of the portal outlined by three flat, pitted-grey stones that lay around an open area of grass and moss. Nature had created a sacred circle on the earth. There I arranged flowers, camellias from my garden, feminine, with rich pink petals and sun-yellow stamen, deep, shiny, surreal colours on the grey stones. I noticed the mystical, golden twilight that was forest light, although it was high noon.

After a few minutes of reverence and peace, I walked through the gateway and climbed steadily, making my way through tough, rubbery supplejack twisted into wire-like baskets. In front of me, I saw the wide trunk of an ancient tree, probably once pukatea, but long ago ascended by a gigantic, parasitic rata vine that had grown into a giant tree on top of the pukatea. The vine celebrated its elevated position in the forest by blooming bright red flowers in the summer months.

After a walk of another thirty minutes, through magnificent rain forest regrowth filled with palms and several varieties of ferns sprouting on rocks and trees, I climbed down to another creek roaring at the bottom of a gully. I stepped onto a stone in the middle of the flowing water and looked up. There, framed in openings between branches, I saw Tāne Mahuta floating above the forest ceiling. I could see a slice of his white trunk, the thick, girth amazingly massive when viewed from my perspective, looking up from the bottom of the watercourse to the high ridge where he lived.

He looked like a scene from *National Geographic*. I could almost hear the naturalist, David Attenborough, narrating with his deep, slightly gravelly voice earned over his eighty-nine years of life: "This is the tree where I first saw kakas, large green forest parrots, which once lived in this valley in their tens of thousands, but are now reduced to an occasional sighting of three or four."

I stooped to the creek and cupped fresh mountain water to my lips, water with the smell of earth and leaves, and a tingle all its own. Over rocks and steps of rock, it tumbled to the river through the rainforest. It was what I drank every day, the greatest blessing possible. However, Tāne beckoned from above.

I slowly ascended the short distance up the creek bank. It was steep, but a few roots provided good hand holds. Climbing my way through vegetation and giant arching roots, I finally stood on the top of the high creek bank. The giant's base was all but lost in the dense vegetation surrounding him, even though it would have taken nine or ten people to encircle him with their hands linked together. I think most people would walk right by the Big Tree without finding him, unless they had seen him from below and were carefully searching. It takes a rain forest to hide something as big as Tāne Mahuta inside it.

Tāne had whiteish-grey undulating roots, which reminded me of massive elephant trunks, soft and curling around one another. I had to step over them, while holding my weight on his buttresses. I worked slowly around him, until I found an opening in Tāne's base, shaped like a small, triangular-shaped cave. I presented the fruits and other gifts I had for the forest god in my backpack, then carefully wedged myself inside him. I was muttering words of gratitude, asking permission, and singing songs when I crawled in. I found him surprisingly hard and strong. This tree was holding a mountain together; it was like being in a whale. I wanted to do more for him, but he was absolutely still: so solid, commanding, and without obvious feeling. Inspired by his example, I quieted my own emotions and mind.

From where I sat in his grotto, I enjoyed a sweeping perspective down the forested valley. His cavern was large enough for me to sit in it cross-legged while looking out over the mountainous expanse of jungle; yet it was a tiny cavity in the base of the old king of the forest. I could see thousands of fern trees, kanuka, pukatea, putaputaweta and other native New Zealand forest dwellers, which covered the steep ridges and deep gullies, descending until they gave out to pasture and the sea in the distance. The few ancient ones like the Big Tree, who had escaped the canopy and were now sky communities, were covered in epiphytes and vines that housed hidden creatures. Out of sight among the forest boughs, bell birds were singing their pure, crystalline temple songs, emitting the purest notes, like Tibetan bells that take you to the center of your heart. I felt my face and my shoulders relax as I recalled why this miracle, the rainforest, was here, but not down there where the pastures began, why the forest was regenerating and not virgin, and why it was still finding its way in a new land of introduced species.

Perhaps Paramena had rested where I was sitting now. Surely this tree was a marvel in his time, too, especially in December when it would have housed thousands of parrots and red blooms. The sawmills didn't get the Big Tree because it would have been impossible to get him down from his steep throne on the mountain. Bessie climbed the hills. Did she sit here? In Paramena's day, before the colonisation of the valley, he would have been spoiled for choice of trees. I knew that Netta and Aroha had sat here. Now national park status had preserved what was left, while rangers trapped the many animals, introduced by the conquest, which threatened the remaining forest.

Sitting inside the Big Tree, I became acutely aware of how much I depended on plants and trees for my existence, every single day I was alive, and with every breath I took. The brilliant green inhaled what I exhaled, and then the green exhaled exactly what I needed to inhale to survive.[21] There are no adequate words to describe the intelligence and constantly evolving perfection of nature, or our profound interrelatedness. Tāne held our world together in a completely motionless stance of great strength and ecological brilliance. I decided I couldn't find a better model for a peaceful living-being than the breath-giving giant living right at my back door.

Tāne proved a divine teacher. What he taught me was that I had to help heal the damage from the past that had taken Tāne's family,

---

[21] A single mature tree can absorb carbon dioxide at a rate of forty-eight pounds a year, and release enough oxygen back into the atmosphere to support two human beings. Trees trap the Sun's energy and transform it into human and animal food, and they provide homes for wildlife. Behind my house on the mountain, they even create weather when the mists come down, and it rains. Every dollar spent on planting and caring for a tree in a city yields benefits that are two to five times that investment—benefits that include cleaner air, lower energy costs, improved water quality, storm water control, and increased property values. See *Trees Pay Us Back: Urban Trees Make a Good Investment*, Pacific Southwest Research Station/USDA Forest Service News Release, 2011.

creeks and streams, hundreds of thousands of birds, and a wild river of estuarine flax. All these features of the Wainui landscape were connected to Tāne, not only by his view from the mountain overlooking the valley, but by the clear creek at his feet, the creek I had crossed to reach him, that ran down to the Wainui River and out into the estuary and the sea. I was reminded that the water cycle is everywhere, including in me. It ran up and down the mountain, then out to the ocean, but not before a little trickle of it ran through our house, which we drank each day, filling us with the essence of Tāne.

9. SPIRITS THAT RULE THE RIVER

*Jars of spring water are not enough anymore.
Take me down to the river.*

— Sufi poet, Jalal al-din Rumi

"IT WAS INEVITABLE," ERNIE SAID, "the day you and your husband bought your land, that you would eventually become active in restoring the riverbank through a dispute with this neighbour. *Judith, how else could the river free itself of cows?* This process will go on until the whole river is clear of animals. It's that simple."

I had returned to Miami to spend time with Ernie Pichardo, my Lucumi teacher. I had taken my adimú to the tree on his advice. Now he was doing a divination reading for me, and I had no idea the impact this reading would have on my life. Ernie had cast the shells and was speaking almost in trance about a Pākehā neighbour in Wainui who had been very difficult. He tried to prevent our access, to buy our land cheaply, he pulled out planted trees, put cows on our land, allowed his cows to foul the river and forest, and much else. We hadn't realized when we bought our land that there were dairy farmers on one side who would not particularly like conservationists.

When Ernie gets serious, he italicizes my name when he addresses me; it's a sort of, *Heads up, this is important, don't miss it,* tone of voice. In Ernie's view, the Wainui River was the director creating the struggle with my neighbour over the riverbank, and it would pull and push the rest of us in accordance with its needs. The river had required this disagreement to protect a sacred site on the riverbank near our home. That the disagreement was about a road and a forest was the realm of Eshu.[22] However, the river itself was vibrating with a different frequency.

"Oshún is inside your river's water," Ernie said. A well-known Lucumí story described the ancient Goddess' ascetic hermitage beside a river in an old growth forest. She had taken only one dress for her hermitage and had lived with profound simplicity. I had pondered this story many times, and it had eventually inspired a vision for my own elder years, which could include meditating by the river, in the forest, like Oshún who had gained enlightenment there.

Oshún is the sweet water of the Earth, quenching our thirsts and purifying our bodies. Her water is the essence of life. Period. There is no life without water, sweet water. I think every one of us has a place inside that melts when we imagine clear, fresh water pouring from a spring on a hillside or swirling by in a river. When we drink water like that, we literally take Oshún into our bodies. Like most adults, my body is fifty to sixty-five percent water. Drinking wild water is like eating wild salmon, a perfection not found in a farmed fish, a city water supply, or a plastic bottle. I can kneel by the edge of our river and dip my palm to drink.

When I go to the riverbank, I think of Oshún and the problems her domain—fresh water—is experiencing throughout the world, including New Zealand, where seventy-five percent of fresh waterways are no longer swimmable because of pollution from the dairy industry. I wonder if Oshún is angry with us. I think about her while I wash my clothes. Her single dress contrasts with the sheer scale of the water contamination that takes place in our world every day: showers with special soaps, conditioners and shampoos, the dish washing, laundry, lawn and home poisons, paints and other chemicals, as well as the millions of tons

---

[22] The Lucumí Orisha are similar to the Māori Atua. Eshu is the trickster god, the translator, and the oldest divinity. Eshu is my guardian Orisha. There is a famous story about Eshu and a road dividing two farmers' fields. He confuses each of them into arguing, and the peace is disrupted through his revelation of the farmers' true hostility toward one another. Eshu is the opener of roads in life and the revealer of hard truths about oneself.

of contaminants from industrial and farming pollution that seep into the ground and ultimately into the water.

We had taken a break for coffee during the reading, and when Ernie returned he promptly said, "Oshún is not the only deity who is important on the Wainui riverbank. There are two other spiritual entities there. One is the *ibubalo do*, elemental riverbank spirits, who play an influential role in a person's initiation. They live there, and wish to speak with you."

"Because of these elemental spirits," Ernie explained, "there is a moist area, vitally alive, the place where Oshún lived during her mystic retreat. A powerful attunement to ashé[23] exists there. Moreover, ibubalo have chosen this spot on the river because they want it made sacred and holy. These spirits are your sources of life, living on the gateway to your land."

The ibubalo do are subtle spirits who protect the riverbank. Their protection is necessary for the life forms, many of which are amphibians, which reside on a riverbank, in the sand and under rocks, nourishing the river and the birds who search for living food there. The endangered whio, blue ducks, are nomads eating riverbank and bottom food, and I've seen one feeding in the sacred pool on the river. Whether we've realized it or not, the riverbank is a very fertile spot where land and water cooperate to nurture a rich neighbourhood of nature spirits, the ibubalo do among them. It is a synergistic relationship between spirits and place. There are many names for the sprites, fairies, nymphs and elves—and, of course, the taniwha who guard rivers and riverbanks.

I was filled with new hope at Ernie's words, because the spot we were talking about was the sacred pool, a mysterious, deep pool on the river. Over the years, this pool had manifested several remarkable events. One was a swirling taniwha pattern that appeared on the day of the spring equinox. The second was an abundant, white flowered clematis vine, blooming just above and hanging down framing the rock face behind the pool, not unnatural, but unusual. The third was a rare

---

[23] Ashe is lifeforce; similar to Māori mauri.

blue duck family that visited the pool when we were quietly watching the water. This was also not unnatural, but very unlikely before this year, when blue ducks were reintroduced to the upper Wainui River. The fourth event was the most mysterious.

On the dawn of the summer solstice, following that spring equinox celebrated with Maki, as the Sun rose above the mountains across from the pool, I spotted a large, flat rock in the shallows, a rock that slowly turned a bright shade of blue. The rock, shaped like an arrowhead, became a soft deep velvety hue, in contrast to the clear greenish water around it. The first rays of light from the Sun struck the rock as the Sun cleared the mountains in the east. I had never noticed anything like this before. I went to the water and laid my hand on the rock. My hand looked normal, with no blue light. The rock felt normal. Yet when I stood again on the river bank, the water around the rock had the same blue cast. I sat watching it until about 10 a.m. As the minutes passed it faded imperceptibly until the blue was gone, returning to its natural granite colour, like the rocks around it. The arrow-shaped rock pointed to the sacred pool. There is probably a natural explanation for this phenomenon, but it wouldn't change the unusual timing and appearance of something I hadn't seen in all the years I've been coming to the sacred pool. The spirits had something to say that day, and they said it in the language of colour. This happened very near the place on the path where the lights appeared years before, while John and I were walking on the river.

"Judith," Ernie continued in his solemn voice, "this sign is very much about the native keepers of the land. It is ancient Māori and a sacred place of worship. You and the people working with you are channels for them. This is where you must acknowledge the ancestral spirits of the Māori, and the indigenous people who came there even before the Māori."

Ernie explained that the Odu showed the ancient Māori carrying out initiations on the riverbank, the way the Yoruba and Lucumí did in West Africa, Cuba and Brazil, where they brought neophytes to spend long, sanctified hours and days on the banks of the sacred river.

They healed past traumas there and were reborn into new hierophant identities. Suddenly, something that had been a mystery for many years became clear to me. The lights that had followed me on the riverbank each night were the ancestors of the Māori people who once lived there. Ernie hadn't known about the white lights that had followed me when I walked on the dark path beside the riverbank. The light was bright behind my back, which I saw as an aureole around my shoulders when I looked right or left, but that hid when I turned to look. It had taken Ernie's reading in Miami for them to reclaim my attention, and for me to appreciate who they were. Now, Ernie said, I needed more gratitude and love for the riverbank spirits and the river, in order for my fortune to be completely positive.

"Rebirth for you will always start on the riverbank," he said. "If your orí (head, destiny) is not responding, go to the riverbank, the source of profound ashé, and there you will revitalize your being." With each word that Ernie spoke, I could feel my energy rising, because everything started to make a strange kind of sense.

This reading of Ernie's—whose main Odu spoke of *victory over strong enemies by the forces that rule the riverbank*—melted any hard separations I had erected between past, present and future, between destiny and free will. If he was right, when we bought our land in Wainui my future was already present in my past, and not just in a metaphorical way. Ernie stressed that this was my destiny; there were no accidents. The river was part of me, like my arms and my legs, and connected to my soul. Wasn't that what I had learned with the little attention I had given to Māori language and spiritualty? Each night for twenty years, when I was in Wainui, I had walked the riverbank when twilight turned to night, feeling the chilly air come down the valley from the waterfall. On the edge of the river, I had watched the top of the giant rata tree disappear into blackness as the last grey ripples flowed over golden sand and granite stones before disappearing in the night.

I think a special destiny chord chimes when we see a place we know we will live, because we are destined to play a role in a drama that will unfold there. I can still remember the day, thirty years ago now, when John, my husband, and I rode over the mountain to look for land. John had picked a spot on a map and said, "Let's go look there."

We stopped the first person we met on the road and asked if any land were for sale. He pointed up to the exact spot John had chosen:

"The owner has just put those acres on the market."

We placed an offer for the land that day. Synchronous experiences are important indicators of positive meaning. My husband and I had something from our destiny files to share on the land we named Waitaha, the water carrier. We both recognized it from the start, although we couldn't have put it into words.

"You took your problem to the riverbank," Ernie continued, "and these entities agreed they would help. Now is the time to return and thank them again, as they are responsible for solving your problem. They are feeling a little neglected. That is why they have finally revealed themselves to you. This Odu," he said, "speaks for the spirits of the riverbank, saying, *You came to me, saw what was wrong, and embraced it. You are welcome here! The other fool is not!* Now, give back thanks."

He then uttered the ultimate insight.

"I want to repeat," Ernie said, his voice rising with emphasis. "This sign is very much about the native keepers of the land. This is their ancestral land. It is a power spot for all who come with respect."

Odu had strikingly portrayed the riverbank and pool as important initiation sites for indigenous people, long before the Europeans arrived, certainly before Paramena, Ngāti Tama, and other Māori tribes. There was a local theory that the ancient Waitaha had passed through and established a wananga, a specialist school for the education of tohunga. When I finally comprehended Ernie's words, a new perspective developed for me: buying our land wasn't a big mistake. It had been my destiny to face the challenges to save the riverbank and pool from cows, to preserve the trees still there, to plant more trees, and, obviously, to honour the sacred water, the ancestors, Tāne and the taniwha. It had taken quite a bit for me to arrive at that conclusion. It's good to have a fifth-dimensional reading from a pro like Ernie.

10. THE CURSE OF WAINUI

What is the appropriate behavior for a man or a woman in the midst of this world, where each person is clinging to his piece of debris? What's the proper salutation between people as they pass each other in this flood?

— Gautama Buddha

IT HAPPENED IN EARLY SUMMER—December in Wainui—after showers had persisted for several days. On the fourth day the rain turned into an insistent, heavy downpour with no wind to carry the storm away. I was in my studio, and only after calling it a day did I notice ankle deep water on the path to the house. Our house was on a slope, and the footpaths around it drained well, except in the largest of rainfalls. John had turned off our hydrowheel the day before in anticipation of a rapid buildup in the size of the creek where our intake was located. Off-grid alternative energy is definitely hands-on, much trickier than plugging into the electric power company's grid. We were ten days away from the longest day in the Southern Hemisphere, and our solar panels should have filled our batteries; but there was zero gain recorded on our control board because of the rain clouds. With the hydro off, too, we were without power, except for what came from a small generator.

Then, without warning, as if it had been just introducing itself before, the storm showed us its true character. Night fell and darkness surrounded us completely. The storm's sound was relentless and terrifying. The river and our surrounding mountain creeks roared like jet engines at London's Heathrow Airport. Sporadically, dislodged rocks and trees crashed into one another, their momentum building as vast quantities of river water rose higher and flowed recklessly faster, rolling giant boulders like stones. The explosive sounds ricocheted from the gullies in the mountains like an advancing army. Throughout the plutonian night I listened, transfixed by the enormous booms and cracks shaking the landscape. My heart beat faster; the fear and anxiety growing within me mirrored the rapid intensification of the rainfall outside—akin to the way the tempest on the heath mirrored the madness of Shakespeare's King Lear as powerful, conflicting emotions tore him apart.

I stayed awake, wide-eyed and frightened, while John slept. Our phone and internet were both out, we had no power, and water dripped down one of the kitchen walls. Around three in the morning, while I was pacing our small lounge, I thought of a boulder in the middle of one of our fields below the house. Its origin and method of arrival were unknown. As I listened to the mayhem outside, I understood how it might have come to be there.

Around 5 a.m. the atmosphere lightened, but the ceiling was very low. Clouds hovered near the ground, and jagged mists lay beneath them. It was like the whole world had been taking a steam bath all night. Ordinarily, heavy rains chisel channels in our long drive that we have to fill with more gravel and dirt, so as the massive cloudbursts slowed to a steady downpour, John and I decided to walk down our gravel driveway to inspect the damage. I donned my rain jacket and wellies. John grabbed his rain gear and a small shovel and followed me. Native trees hung over our long driveway. It led to the entrance lane we had made along the riverside tree reserve, a lane that ran across the short valley to the highway. I had been certain our driveway would have deep ruts running with water. To my happy surprise, water was still running smoothly in the drains we had dug the day before.

However, the angel of death had not bypassed us completely. When I was a hundred meters from the bottom of our driveway, I could hear water roaring. I had to know the truth. I raced down the rest of the way to the gate, which is across from the river. There our entrance lane travels along the river for a half mile to the highway. When I reached the gate, I came to an abrupt stop, transfixed by the terrifying sight in front of me. White-capped waters raged past, filling the lower part of the valley, carrying trees and big pieces of landslips, which whizzed by in the dangerously swift current. With mounting alarm, I realized that our riverbank reserve, with its trees, the four-foot-tall fence, and our almost one kilometre sand lane to the highway *were gone. Vanished.* In place of them was a vast, white, roiling river, charging for the ocean. A large uprooted tree flew by in front of me. Dazed, I walked back up the drive to the place where John had stopped to clear a ditch with his small, red shovel. He saw me coming and called out.

"Wow, the drive still looks pretty good," he said enthusiastically.

"Honey," I said, when I got closer to him, not wanting to shout and alarm him, because that would happen soon enough. "We're going to need a lot more than your little shovel."

He saw the look on my face, dropped the shovel, and quickly followed me down to the gate. Silently, we watched the formerly small and gentle Wainui River roar past us, an implacable field of rapids, floating trees, boulders and sand. We were both too shocked to have any idea what to do. It is my experience that when a natural disaster strikes, it is always unexpected; therefore, it is by definition, a shocking event, for which you are unprepared emotionally and mentally. The windless rain started to fall hard again; it rolled off my forehead and chin. We felt disoriented because it was impossible to tell the time of day. The day should have been bright and blue. Instead, the low, fuliginous cloud cover had hidden the dawn, which had happened some time before, creating a grey world without markers. It was a water world gone mad.

We quickly walked back to the house, where we decided we needed to find out what was happening to the rest of Wainui Bay. We had to discover if anything was left beyond the roaring river and the giant landslides. We should have taken a lunch as well as my camera, because a walk that ordinarily takes a half hour turned into a five-hour marathon through horrendous destruction and constant rain.

The only way to walk was across the land of our neighbour, the farmer who detested John and me. Crossing his higher pasture, we felt uneasy and shaken as we made our escape to the highway. Approaching the road, we saw the Wainui River, fast-flowing water, thick mud, debris and sand, streaming across the highway and onto the pasture, where an enormous lake had formed. The lake appeared to run all the way to the estuary. We now understood that the river, ordinarily the size of a ribbon, had grown monstrously, and scooped up tons and tons of natural materials along its path of ruin. In the surrounding hills, we could see where scores of enormous landslides had deposited broad, tumbling mounds of watery debris. The highway, which had lost big pieces of its tar-seal, floated down the great lake in front of us. Walking was treacherous, because we had to climb large piles of fallen hillside that were muddy and very soft in places, like quicksand. Most of the land in Wainui is composed of golden, granite sand that collapses easily, especially in places where the land had been overgrazed for years and no replanting done.

When we finally reached the milking shed across the highway, we encountered desolate wreckage: a farm building half under sand and water, machines buried, fences gone. A group of people from the local commune were walking from the other direction, looking as wet, muddy and muddled as we were.

"What does it look like down your way?" we asked.

"About the same as here. No one was injured, but it was close. A dam of logs coming down the stream broke about midnight and nearly swamped us in its wake."

They had no mobile or landline connections, but they confirmed the road was closed. Our beautiful valley, with its mountains, estuary and bay, which I had always thought looked like a temperate Tahiti, was devastated. Never, never underestimate the power of nature was my only thought, and it revolved, again and again, like a broken record.

The highway into Wainui was almost destroyed, and there was no other exit. However, the day after the flood contractors managed to open a small passage for vehicles in order to move the farmer's cows, which needed milking. Before the day was over, three hundred cows or more went over a narrow single lane in the back of a contractor's truck. Then, for the next two weeks, the police led convoys over the mountain road so we could shop and see friends and family. When we could travel unescorted, no one except residents was permitted to enter Wainui, so few knew how badly it was damaged. When I first drove behind the police, over the mountain highway, I was shocked to see what the contractor had risked to open the road for the cows. Giant monsoon slides blocked it, and in two places the small two-lane highway plunged hundreds of meters to the sea, leaving only a vehicle-wide passageway.

Three floods, more minor in scope, but destructive nonetheless, occurred over the next two months. Only gradually did I realize that our valley had been greatly altered for the foreseeable future. The long scars on the mountains looked ugly and violent. And the river flowed everywhere until an army of contractors contained it behind a stone embankment. After that, it no longer seemed part of our landscape, sacrificed to the need for pasture, rather than a free river that would overflow its banks in flood. A river needs a riverbank, and now, where the embankment was built, there was none. According to Ernie, the riverbank is the most spiritually alive place on a river. Only the stretch of the river on the reserve and in the park retained its wild, biodiverse character. Prior to the river's enclosure in the embankment, it had flooded and then receded across the pastures, causing little damage. By contrast, this flood, called a one-in-five-hundred-year event, had caused mammoth damage.

Once upon a time, when there was a river of flax in Wainui, the flax had controlled floods and erosion. Called harakeke by Māori, flax was a symbol of family. They wove it into utensils, houses, ropes and warm clothing, and used it as medicine and food. The nectar-filled flowers fed the iconic bellbirds and tuis. Harakeke stabilized riverbanks and helped restore plant biodiversity after floods.[24] Now, rather than harakeke, the engineers' stone walls and introduced willow contained the river. The farmer spent months digging more drainage canals across

---

[24] These restore plant biodiversity and help protect the environment, for example, by stabilising riverbanks. Flax can be propagated from seed or by dividing off small fans of leaves and planting them directly in the soil. It belongs to the hemerocal-

his pastures, which were former wetlands, as well as constantly digging out his drains after a heavy rain, when riparian plantings of harakeke would have helped considerably. And without plantings, the waste from his cattle business flowed through the granite sand soils, and soon ended up in the river and estuary, as does cattle waste all over Aotearoa. These farmers were working against the natural order that prevented erosion: flax on wetlands and thick rain forest on the hills.

Ordinarily, in Wainui we receive ninety inches of rain a year. However, during these torrential rains we received over thirty-nine inches of rain in fewer than forty-eight hours, the largest single rainfall event ever recorded in New Zealand. Throughout the years we had lived in Wainui, the river had never jumped its banks to cause more than temporary flooding. This storm was different—an example of the kind of extreme weather that climate scientists predict will become more frequent as greenhouse gasses trap more moisture in the atmosphere. The forest on our land and in the park remained sodden for months, and a moist haze obscured the sky most of the summer. The light felt weak and cool, and nothing in our garden would grow. Tāne, the big tree behind our house, sat on the edge of the creek, which had swollen into a river. We could walk to him over a huge swathe of clear land in the forest, seeing him long before we reached him. He was still monumental on the edge of the high creek bank, but he was now exposed and visible, because all the lower vegetation was gone. Despite his size, Tāne looked vulnerable.

When a friend offered her apartment in Miami for six months, we welcomed the chance to escape. As we arrived in Miami, I felt like a refugee, muddled and traumatized by the gut-wrenching despoliation of our valley. The experience slept inside me, though outside I revelled

---

lidaceae family and the phormium genus. It grows naturally only in New Zealand and Norfolk Island—no other country has produced a plant quite like it. In Māori sayings and songs flax is often a metaphor for family bonds and human relationships. It is also a national emblem, and used in logos for local and government organizations. Although flax has been exported, it is a plant that many New Zealanders associate strongly with their homeland.

in the Miami sunshine with friends and family. Anyone who has been through a natural disaster knows how it separates you from those who haven't, and multiplies by many times what you have to do every day. However, escaping to Miami also meant I could consult Ernie immediately to find out what was going on.

Ernie touched the shells to my forehead and hands. I closed my eyes and listened to my inhalation and exhalation. I thought it would be a few minutes, but Ernie did not delay or ask qualifying questions. As soon as he saw the sign, he began translating its meaning for me.

The odu that had fallen on his mat was *Ogundá*, containing blessings that were not firm, and I soon learned about its dire predictions. A number of Orisha were involved. They spoke of a never-ending battle between Shangó and Ogún, represented by the elements of fire and iron. I immediately thought of the army of farmers with their tractors, diggers, slashers and bulldozers, who had shown up a month after the flood to help move tons of wreckage and logs from the farm land. They pushed the wood together in huge mounds. Much of this was a result of clear-felling a large number of pine trees that had grown on the hills above the pasture. Then the farmer torched the piles of wood on his land, without permission, and without regard to their potential uses or the immense amount of carbon their burning sent into the air. After his work, the sky was masked by opaque mist and caliginous smoke. When we had left Wainui, it truly resembled the aftermath of apocalypse. I didn't have to think very hard to relate to what Ernie said about fire and iron.

"The odu applies to the water, too," Ernie continued. "We are talking about the purification of the arteries of the Earth. The odu says this applies here, because the flow in the Wainui River is being disrupted, and there is a challenge in the water itself."

Ernie explained Ogundá is an Earth odu that incorporates the idea of toxic intrusion, such as fertilizers, weed killers and cow manure. The landslides had also filled the river with sand, clay, trees and broken masses of vegetation.

"The water is struggling." Ernie raised his voice, as he does, to make important points. "Its ability to circulate is challenged 24/7. This includes all that run-off of junk from the land and a re-shaping of things. I'd be more comfortable in saying ... *the flood is not the problem!* The problem is what has been done to the artery. It is ill and needs a doctor. Not a malpractice doctor! They've been fooling around with this river and its flow in different ways, so its circulation is messed up. And rather than doing something where we could legitimately say people were sustainably employed, we find human greed and the mentality of control."

In this odu, the situation was very serious, because Ernie was also talking about sea levels moving higher and covering the land as the sea pushed back against the natural flow of the river. The domain of the Orisha Oyá, the tempest and the storm, was also active, eroding the sides of the river and creeks, throwing sand and mud into the arteries of the land. Ernie's interpretation of this odu increasingly sounded like the executive director of the Sierra Club talking about habitat destruction, water pollution and climate change. Ernie said he could see in the odu that the farmer's family were people who were financially well-off when they settled in Wainui.

"If they had established a business in harmony with the environment and hadn't altered the place in any significant manner, they would have been okay." He added this applied all the way down their ancestral line to the people living today.

"*They did not count on the sacredness of Wainui*," Ernie emphasised. "Unless the owners embrace the valley as sacred and restore as much as possible, they will continue to suffer. According to the odu, Wainui will never be the same. There is no hope for complete restoration, but you and the others still have to do what is possible.

"If the humans think that their riches, their science, logic and power as humans can be superior to that sacred land and the ancestors there who are spirits—good luck! I am very certain they will lose all their riches. And they are going to lose this place. *The ancestors are dead people. They have all the time in the world!* So this is not a fight the farmer can outlive and win. He is *not* going to win."

As so many times before, Ernie was definite and confident. He predicted major financial losses, all driven by "humankind's wickedness and maliciousness." I interjected that some people thought the farmer was a "nice" bloke.

"That's the point," Ernie said, leaning over his desk toward me. "It is the effect of the wickedness of his ancestors, as well as him. He may be nice, Judith, but take your emotional nonsense out of this. He is doing wrong knowingly or unknowingly. He is either innocent, but acting in the wrong way, or he knows exactly what he is doing, and is still acting in the wrong way. It doesn't matter. The ancestors don't care that this gentleman may be a nice human being ... *his actions are wrong on that sacred land.*"

Ernie's view was that the land and the ancestors did not care whether the farmer was nice because nice is not what the land and the ancestors needed. Ernie was adamant the farmer should have the maturity to sit down and rethink his whole approach to the land. This would be taking positive advantage of the current crisis to reevaluate a blatantly wrong direction. Otherwise, Ernie said, it would be a total loss, and many deleterious things would happen.

"If he wants to be hardheaded, he can be that way all he wants. He is not bigger than the ancestors. That is the wrong fight for him to take. This is when we say, that land is cursed!"

Because of blockages on the estuary around the river's mouth, the river had flooded again and again, each time with much smaller rains. These floods didn't much affect our road, but the farmer's low-lying land still filled with water where an estuary of flax once grew, and winds had thrown trees over his fences. During one minor flood, his whole effluent system was damaged. In fact, from the time of the great storm until the time of this reading, I felt the land, air and river were altered in ominous ways. Remember Cate Blanchett at the beginning of the first *Lord of the Rings* movie, when she prognosticated in her deep, rich voice, *"The world is changed"*?

Scenes from the film were shot on the mountain above my land. I had felt Blanchett's words inside, and spoken them out loud; they had become like a mantra to me. Our rainfall was the highest ever, the river was constrained behind stone walls, and over one hundred land slips disfigured our valley. When we glance at the newspaper, we see new climate disruption records daily. The world is changed. This rapacious way of human life around the globe, not just in New Zealand, is obviously at an end—and the Dilogún agrees.

Ernie's reading in Miami about the dairy land and the flood sent me thinking in entirely different ways about the Wainui Valley. He was right. Real restoration of the environment once found in Wainui would take millennia of undisturbed regrowth and the resumption of evolutionary speciation. Aotearoa evolved a unique flora and fauna isolated from the rest of the world. It could not be magically recreated. Yet we had to restore what we could.

11. RECHARGING THE LAND

*You are the one who must build the fire.
Don't expect spirits to put on flesh
and do it for you. You are their hands.*
— Ernesto Pichardo

FIVE MONTHS AFTER THE FLOOD READING, and just before returning to Aotearoa, I visited Ernie again, making the long drive from the apartment in crowded Brickell near downtown Miami to his home way south of Miami, where there was still a little green space. We had a lot to say before entering the consultation room; it was a long wind-down and goodbye talk. When I finally sat in the chair across the desk from my padrino, I needed to relax. Ernie gestured to the shells on the mat as he spoke.

"You have blessings and complete support from an egun (spirit) in a foreign land. She wants to be like a mother to you. If you have any issue, even like border-line hysteria, she'll come and help you. This can be the most constructive and nourishing relationship of mother and child. She sees what you have done and wants to have a reciprocal relationship with you. Whatever you can do for her will be welcome, because she's in your ancestral core now. You must treat her like a mother, and she will come in and bless you." Ernie tapped the shells as he spoke and smiled.

I sat up straighter. This was unexpected—a direction I had not anticipated. Never before had a spirit come through so strongly with protection and blessings, especially at a time when I was feeling low.

I began to name people while Ernie checked with the shells to verify an identity. We knew she was female, deceased, and from a place far away. I thought it was Thelma, the aunt of my godson's father, who was a Māori singer. I have Thelma's amber necklaces on my altar. No, it wasn't Thelma. Finally, Ernie identified Netta as my guide. She was Aroha's mother, Netta, who had suffered so much in her life.

When I finally left, I returned to our apartment, lit a candle, and talked to Netta, because it felt right and because I required her help. Among other things, I was worried about Aroha and needed Netta's assistance to find her. I also had a problem and asked Netta to send someone with the answer. My first response came the next day, when Aroha turned out to be in Rarotonga. I'd had no idea where she was, and she let me know she was okay. Over the next few months, I was surprised by the genuine support and the uplifting of my spirit. I also felt more and more connected with Aroha.

Netta must have appeared to help me carry out the Māori ancestral mission for the land. The way Ernie saw it, the land in Wainui was a constant reminder to the dead of their defeat. He said, "A spirit thinks,

Oba Ernesto Pichardo

'I died a hundred years ago, and my land is still being dominated by the same people.'"

I could only imagine how strongly Netta would be feeling about this, as she was the person who taught her daughter about what had happened to the Māori under British subjugation.

Ernie said the ancestral spirits were roaming the land and hills, and seeing the conqueror and his practices that were harming the forests, the water and the land. Their conquest of nature continued unabated. He said wave after wave of conquerors were there together in spirit, not necessarily getting along, but in agreement about the condition of their people. And then came their most important advice to the living.

"We are here," they said, "and there is a path out of this which *begins with recharging the land* in a way that is true to the old traditions."

Ernie said that Netta and the spirits who came with her had authority for this, and they would see that it came about. The regeneration should begin with small things that the Māori ancestral spirits would recognise. Most important, Ernie said, was to use native flora and to plant them extensively, so the spirits who showed up could identify with familiar plants that grew in Wainui when Netta and her own ancestors lived there. Māori people had to be in the forefront of this regeneration, because they had to break the state of colonisation that still existed in each and every mind. They must take control of their illness in order to heal from it. In Ernie's view, it was all about *their* healing, and that healing had to be connected back to the land.

Soon after this reading, I returned to Waitaha. Aroha had come back from Rarotonga. She had once been my neighbour, but had departed long ago on her spiritual journey around the world, especially through the Pacific Islands where her ancestors had lived before their waka carried them to Aotearoa. She could trace her genealogy to Tahiti, Rarotonga and to Rapanui. I had accompanied her on her quest to the sacred island of Raiatea, in French Polynesia, where there were megalithic stone monuments, once the sacred meeting places of the Maohi people, ancestors of the Māori peoples who today live in Aotearoa and

Rarotonga. These Polynesians traversed the oceans on double-hulled vessels with sails, steering by the stars and the complex wave motion of the water, and using other natural signs. Polynesia is the world's largest country, if we count the area it occupied in the Pacific before it was fragmented by whalers, traders, missionaries and colonialists.

Aroha and I now felt closer than ever, since her mother Netta was our common spirit guide. Netta had practised traditional Māori arts and crafts. She taught Aroha the arts of weaving with harakeke, as well as rope making, once used for the outrigger boats that sailed the seas. She also taught Aroha to question the Pākehā hegemony in Aotearoa. Immediately after we talked to Netta, interesting things opened for us. As the weeks went on, we came to trust the source, although we still had to do the work.

Aroha weaving flax

I thought it would be interesting for Aroha to have a reading with Ernie to resolve a dilemma she was facing. Maybe it would also clarify more of what we could do in Wainui to lift the curse of our poisoned lands and water. Ernie had been doing Skype readings with his clients for a while, so we decided to try it. I didn't tell him anything about Aroha or Netta. I pulled up my Skype on the computer. When Ernie answered the call, I introduced him to Aroha. We chatted for a while before he asked her to light a candle and place a clear glass of water next to the computer, where she would see and speak with him. After that, he threw the shells for a long time. We could see him gazing out the window of his divination office in Miami. Aroha said later his glasses glinted in the sunlight, and she could see on his lenses silhouettes of the trees outside in his garden.

"Okay, well, your Mom is here," Ernie finally announced. He hadn't looked at the shells, and I could see that he was simply channeling his spirit guide, not looking for an odu.

"Your Mom says she is at the forefront of this life-cycle taking you to a new place. She's in charge, and she is moving forward. It is her authority to do it, and it is her creation. I see her right here. I see her standing, not sitting, next to water, maybe a river, and she is right at the riverbank. It's night-time, not daytime. I see her creating a fire pit. There's a hanging pot on a tripod over the fire. I see smoke, lots of smoke. And I see her moving, reaching into the small iron pot. She picks it up and passes it around like she is burning incense, but it's not incense!

"I see her in a long skirt that goes to the floor and covers her feet, and she's wearing a blouse that is colorful. The skirt is white and her blouse doesn't have a collar. It's long-sleeved and has colors like rainbows. She has long hair, but it is held back by something similar to a scarf. She's making sure the smoke is getting into the wind. She is creating *dense* smoke. What she's doing is *purifying* that area. She's pushing away all the negativity. Does that make sense?

"Aroha, what she's showing me is what she wants you to do to further detox this contaminated space. She wants you to do this *right now*! She says, '*Put your faith on us*', meaning your mother and those spirits coming with her. As long as you are convinced without doubt of their presence and their authority, that's your strength. As long as you hold on to that, they will be enabled to move things forward in the right direction; but you are the one who must build the fire. Don't expect spirit to put on flesh and do it for you. You are their hands."

I had no idea what Ernie was talking about and wondered what Aroha thought. She cried during most of his reading, and then, after a pause, surprised me with her words.

"I've been thinking about doing this for a long time," Aroha said in a soft voice. "I know just what my mother is doing."

"My mother, Netta" she continued, "often ran away from our home when she was fed up with life. She would go to a private Māori place on the water where she could do our Māori cultural practices, like weaving, painting and making medicine. One thing she often did was to make a healing balm called rangoa, which she gave to the people around her to harmonise her environment. I made this many times with her when I was a child."

Aroha said Netta wore a long white apron and many-colored scarves like rainbows around her neck and hair when she was preparing these medicines; this ensemble exactly fit the description of the spirit in Ernie's vision. She also used an iron pot like Ernie had described. As I soon discovered, the cooking method he articulated, and the dense smoke that was produced while moving the pot around and standing by the water, were all quite accurate, too. Ernie had repeated this medicine *must be made soon*! He spoke with absolute certainty, and insisted Aroha get busy.

"Move on it!" he urged. "Do it now! This will clear the air for the next cycle. The moment you unite with the ancestors, you become an empowered source that supersedes and overcomes the obstructions and negativity that exist. I think your Mom is asking, 'Where's your soul? Is it on vacation somewhere? Take it back. It's yours.' She's walking around the river; she's not going anywhere. With her are other spirits. They are still walking around too. They're saying, '*Get your soul back, so you can reconnect to the soul of the land.*'"

A few days later, Aroha and I went alone to the sacred pool. When we first climbed down the steep bank and stood on the shore, two white-faced herons flew up the river right in front of us. I watched the birds glide by—two of them, two of us.

We were in front of the pool, which was a clear green that day, calm with its distinctive whirl of water. Aroha was dressed in a long, white sarong and white blouse, with many rainbow-colored scarves wrapped around her neck and waist, the same clothes she had seen her mother Netta wear many times. Despite the cool day and the setting sun, she was barefoot. I was dressed in my usual light pants and white shirt, with sparkling fresh water pearls around my neck. We were there to make rangoa, the healing balm that Ernie saw her mother making on the riverbank.

Our first job was to pick leaves from the kawakawa trees[25] on my land. We filled Aroha's iron pot to the brim with their dark green foliage, pressing them down to make more room. I could smell the peppery kawakawa as I crushed it beneath my hands. I often chewed the leaves while I walked around our land; they clear the mouth with a refreshing taste. Aroha says that Netta used to tell her to pick the leaves with insect holes, because those were obviously the tastiest.

After gathering kawakawa, Aroha and I collected wood and stones along the riverbank. She built a stone trivet to hold her pot, while I started a fire with small kindling. The fire caught quickly. Soon the flames heated the iron pan that Aroha held over them. She then set it on the stone trivet. When her pan was hot, she added a large lump of beeswax and stirred it until it melted. When it was liquid, she added an equal amount of coconut oil, which was almost as solid as the bees' wax because of the cool temperature. When the two melted together, it was time to add the green kawakawa leaves. She stirred them into the bubbling oil.

We had already laid kumara on a sand circle, facing north, south,

---

[25] Kawakawa, a member of the pepper family and related to kava, is one of the Māori's most traditional and useful medicinal plants.

east and west, as an offering for the Māori ancestors. The Māori introduced kumara to Aotearoa in the thirteenth century. Oral history tells of canoe voyagers travelling back to ancestral lands to bring home more varieties of this tasty and nutritious sweet potato. The Waitaha, Aroha's tribal peoples, were expert kumara gardeners and navigators. When we offered the kumara, a nutritious, ceremonial and ancestral food, it carried the sense of the whole Polynesian nation and its journeys over the sea. I laid more kumara in the giant roots of the old rata tree, which, despite the flood, still stood over the sacred pool.

During the deluge, when the river had been forced over the riverbank by a giant slide of sand, mud and trees, the sacred pool had emptied itself, along with five or six feet of sand. When the river bottom was exposed, we could see the previously hidden lower six feet of rock wall on the opposite shore. There, a yoni, a stylized drawing of female genitals, was revealed, a long, vertical cleft in the rock, which was normally concealed by sand and water. Ernie had divined that Oshún was in the water: it was as if the water disappeared just long enough to reveal the universal symbol of woman to prove his point.

Ernie had seen a lot of smoke on the river in his vision of Netta, and Aroha knew just what he meant. However, I was still astonished to see smoke finally curl out of the pot when the kawakawa leaves turned dark in the boiling green liquid. Aroha swung the pot back and forth until there was a large amount of smoke, dense smoke as Ernie had seen, turning in slow circles as it rose over the river. She stirred vigorously to keep the rangoa from burning, and soon tested the balm on the back of her hand, which she passed under my nose. It was sweet smelling, like honey and spicy kawakawa. The rangoa had congealed into a waxy unguent, the soft color of forest leaves with a fresh aroma, subtle and relaxing like lavender.

Finally, it was just right, and Aroha poured the fragrant emollient into small jars. She had specific recipients in mind for each of these, people Aroha wished to salute with this sacred gift inspired by her mother, Netta. Ernie had described the proper recharging of the land in Wainui, but first the ancestors needed to see familiar acts, like making rangoa on the river. This would anchor them to the land and help *spur* its regeneration.

We climbed the riverbank when the Sun set and darkness covered the water. It was cold by then, and we needed to get back to the house. The precious rangoa in its small jar felt warm in my pocket as we walked up the lane through the forest and home. It was the first time since the flood I had felt something besides grief or lethargy on the river. The riverbank was in a resting mode, healing and transitional, her scars still visible: dead trees, other trees half dead and dying slowly, naked slashes on the steep hills, and a new lane and path enclosed by a fence on top of the old one where the river had buried it beneath the sand.

I imagined I now knew what happened when Oshún became angry: a giant flood whose waters become a great, destructive force. However, the cycle was turning again, and during our rangoa making I saw there was new life everywhere. Thickets of deep green tree tutu and manuka were regenerating around the other native trees we had planted, and hundreds of foxgloves, almost in bloom, filled the enormous landslide just upstream of the sacred pool.

A forest reaches climax after an unimaginably long time. If we include the birds our forest once held, many ground-dwelling, flightless species in vast numbers and sizes, as well as songbirds and nectar eaters full of flight, the evolutionary time scale expands even further. Wainui cannot be restored, because the virgin forest and scores of bird, invertebrates and fish species are extinct; but we can do what is possible. Tūhoe believe that Tāne Mahuta, the giant tree father of life in the forest, withdrew the mauri (life force) when they lost the spiritual mana of their own tribe during the colonial land grab and its violent aftermath. They say that once their culture was destroyed, and no longer supported by their prayers and rituals, Tāne drained the life force from the native birds, which is why today they were still declining.[26]

My new spiritual perspective allows me to credit both the spiri-

---

[26] Lyver et al.: *Tūhoe Tuawhenua Mātauranga of Kererū 7, New Zealand Journal of Ecology* (2008) 32 (1): 7-17 ©New Zealand Ecological Society. Available on-

tual Māori view for the birds' decline, as well as the scientific view that habitat loss and foreign predators have wreaked the havoc on them. In any case, it is clear that it's impossible to separate our salvation on this planet from the forest and from the forest birds. All life is important, but if the trees and the birds are protected, most other life forms will survive healthfully. Therefore, it is not only the forest we must restore in Wainui, it is the forest's animation: the songs, dances, flights and antics of its birds (which are ancient present-time dinosaurs) that bring to life everything around them.

For all these reasons, I now nurture, among others, endangered, ground-dwelling wekas, our own little feathered dinosaurs, recently reintroduced by the Department of Conservation after they disappeared in the 1980s due to predation, disease and habitat destruction. I observe their social and family life, offer them extra food, and learn their sounds, which vary from an intense churring with their babies to occasional calls between the parents, who mate for life. When parents are separated, they stretch their necks, pointing to the heavens, and open their bills with a full-throated, loud and repetitive cry across the forest and land. They call and respond; then other birds answer from the surrounding forest.

When the female of our oldest couple, Ms. E, lost a toe to a hunter's trap, her partner of eight years fed her deep in the bushes for several weeks. As I write, she is still alive and has three new chicks. The birds vary so much from one another. We have names for many of them, the ones who stick around and talk to us: Split Tail, Sly, Mr. Wee, and his son Weeji, his partner, Jump, Mr. Big and Ms. Egg (B & E), and several others. When I return from the village, they call to me and I answer in their tongue. They flock to the car to see if I have an egg for them, then follow me to the house.

I've never seen a weka, nor any other wild bird, overeat. Dogs and cats will eat beyond hunger and become huge; and we know humans

---

line: http://www.newzealandecology.org/nzje/Tūhoe Tuawhenua mātauranga of kererū (Hemiphaga novaseelandiae novaseelandiae) in Te Urewera.

often overeat as a pastime or indulgence. By contrast with our own species, wekas eat with gusto for a minute or two, then return to foraging. They are nomads, like the original people who lived here, feeding on worms and other forest creatures while they travel, which explains why they check out new plantings where land is disturbed. They are very successful, intelligent, strategising nomads. I recently saw a weka with a fresh water crawfish in its claw, pulling off the crustacean's head, making an excellent meal in the tumbling creek. Now I wait for their arrival each day, and I miss them terribly when they are away on their nomadic forest walks. Every night they play, racing and fighting without hurting one another, flapping their small wings. When I see one of our weka, I simply smile.

I remember what Ernie said, that Wainui can never be the former paradise it was before the colonial invasions. Yet, we can do what is possible, love what is here, and give thanks. Luckily, I'm not in charge, and none of this is under my control. The process of renewal is led by the world of spirit, which wants to see familiar ancient practices reenacted on the river. The ancestors also want native plants, trees and birds restored, the flora and fauna from the time before the British arrived.

Weka adult, Mr Big, caring for his chicks

RECHARGING THE LAND

There are many ways this is happening, and many ways for even apartment dwellers to get involved, all the groups, organizations, iwi, clubs, predator free areas that need volunteers, too many to name. There is no stopping the restoration now; there is only going forward without too much conflict, which we Homo sapiens love.

Aroha and I brought together past, present and future as we cooked Māori medicine on the river, watched over by Netta and the ancestors who came with her. Ernie and Aroha, Lucumí and Māori, walked backwards into the future. They both placed importance on seeking guidance for future actions from the wisdom of past ancestral deeds and mythical heroes. Through Ernie's vision, we looked into the past, when Netta was making rangoa, then walked into our future, where we found ourselves making the same rangoa in the present. Once I knew my guide as the bright, white light at my back when I walked by the riverbank in the dark of the night. Now I knew it had been Māori ancestors, who were leading the purification of this ancient and beautiful land.

As for me, who makes this journey, I also feel the purification inside. The journey is about life after death, about spirits, and especially about the spirit of nature; of natural places that are powerful and special. I want the mauri to dwell in our land, in our birds, and I want to praise it, thank it, and be in union with it. I know that this powerful and divine thing will give attention to everybody: there are no castes, titles, classes, races or genders recognized in a natural state of being. When I walk the river to the waterfall and back, I can sense veriditas, that sacred force in perpetual motion. It is inside my heart, my soul, my voice. And when I take time to adore it, my inner self mirrors its beauty and elation.

GLOSSARY

MĀORI *

Aotearoa	The Māori name for New Zealand.
Awa	River, stream, creek.
Atua	Ancestor with continuing influence, god, demon, supernatural being, deity, ghost, object of superstitious regard, strange being. Many Māori trace their ancestry from atua in their whakapapa and they are regarded as ancestors with influence over particular domains.
Harakeke	New Zealand flax, *Phormium tenax*—an important native plant with long, stiff, upright leaves and dull red flowers. Found on lowland swamps throughout Aotearoa New Zealand. It has straight, upright seed pods.
Heke	To migrate, move.
Iwi	Tribe, nation, a large group of people descended from a common ancestor and associated with a distinct territory.
Kahikatea	White pine, *Dacrycarpus dacrydioides*—a tall coniferous tree of mainly swampy ground, the leaves are scale-like and soft to touch.
Kākā	*Nestor meridionalis*—large native forest parrot with olive-brown and dull green upperparts and crimson underparts.
Karanga	To call, call out, shout, summon.
Kawakawa	Pepper tree, *Macropiper excelsum*—a small, densely-

---

* Most of the Māori definitions are adapted from the Māori Dictionary, online version.

	branched tree with heart-shaped leaves. Found throughout the North Island and as far south as Banks Peninsula. Used for ceremonies, including removing tapu, for medicinal purposes.
Kererū	New Zealand pigeon, *Hemiphaga novaeseelandiae*—a large green, copper and white native bush pigeon which was eaten by Māori.
Kuia	Elderly woman, grandmother, female elder.
Mahinga kai	Garden, cultivation, food-gathering place.
Manuka	Tea-tree, *Leptospermum scoparium*—a common native scrub bush with aromatic, prickly leaves and many small, white, pink or red flowers.
Mauri	Life principle, life force, vital essence, special nature, a material symbol of a life principle, source of emotions—the essential quality and vitality of a being or entity.
Mihi	To greet, pay tribute, acknowledge, thank.
Ngai Tahu	Tribal group of much of the South Island.
Ngarara Huarau	One name of a Wainui taniwha, which is found elsewhere in Aotearoa.
Pa	Fortified village, fort, stockade, screen, blockade, city.
Pākehā	English, foreign, European, exotic—introduced from or originating in a foreign country.
Papatūānuku	Earth, Earth mother and wife of Rangi-nui—all living things originate from them.
Pounamu	Greenstone, a type of jade, found on the South Island, which has healing and other sacred properties.
Rangatira	To be of high rank, become of high rank, ennobled, rich, well off, noble, esteemed, revered.
Rangi	Sky, sky god.
Rongoā	Remedy, medicine, drug, cure, medication, treatment, solution (to a problem), tonic.
Rātā	*Metrosideros robusta* (Northern), *Metrosideros umbellata* (Southern)—large forest tree with crimson flowers and hard red timber. The Northern rātā is a strangling he-

GLOSSARY

	miepiphyte that sends roots from the canopy that thicken and fuse into an independent trunk, which eventually becomes a tall free-standing tree.
Tāne-Mahuta	Atua of the forests and birds and one of the children of Rangi-nui and Papa-tū-ā-nuku.
Tangata whenua	Local people, hosts, indigenous people—people born of the whenua, i.e. of the placenta and of the land where the people's ancestors have lived and where their placenta are buried.
Taniwha	Water spirit, monster, dangerous water creature, powerful creature, chief, powerful leader, something or someone awesome—taniwha take many forms from logs to reptiles and whales and often live in lakes, rivers or the sea. They are often regarded as guardians by the people who live in their territory, but may also have a malign influence on human beings.
Taringa	Ear.
Te Ika-a-Māui	North Island.
Te reo	The Māori language.
Te Waipounamu	The South Island, where the sacred pounamu is found.
Tohunga	Skilled person, chosen expert, priest, healer—a person chosen by the agent of an atua and the tribe as a leader in a particular field because of signs indicating talent for a particular vocation.
Totara	*Podocarpus totara*, *Podocarpus cunninghamii*—large forest trees with prickly, olive-green leaves not in two rows. Found throughout Aotearoa/New Zealand.
Urupā	Burial ground, cemetery, graveyard.
Wai	Water.
Wananga	School.
Weka	Woodhen, *Gallirallus australis greyi*, *Gallirallus australis australis*—a brown-feathered endemic bird streaked with black with a short bill and legs, able to run fast but flightless.

Whakapapa	Genealogy, genealogical table, lineage, descent—reciting whakapapa was, and is, an important skill and reflects the importance of genealogies in Māori society in terms of leadership, land and fishing rights, kinship and status.
Whakatauki	Proverb, aphorism.
Whanganui	A river and tribal group in the central North Island; the first natural body to be given legal status in New Zealand law courts.
Whānau	Extended family, family group, a familiar term of address to a number of people—the primary economic unit of traditional Māori society. In the modern context the term is sometimes used to include friends who may not have any kinship ties to other members.

LUCUMI

Ashé	Similar to *kundalini* in yoga and *chi* in Taoist philosophy. Ashé is the universal energy of birth, evolution and enlightenment. It is heard in Lucumí greetings and prayers to affirm and invoke awareness.
Adimú	A small offering of food for orisha and/or ancestral spirits.
Dilogún	A shortened form of the Yoruba word *merindilogún*, which means sixteen. It refers to the sixteen cowrie shells used in this ancient method of divination.
Egun	The spirit of a deceased person.
Elegguá/Eshu	The prime mover of the universe, this complex orisha is a profound philosopher and translator of the Dilogún.
Ifá	The formal Yoruba divination system used by babaláwo, who divine with sixteen palm nuts or a divination chain.
Lucumí	The word Lucumí was a greeting used by the Yoruba people in Cuba to recognize their common ancestry. Now it refers to the sect of Yoruba religion that began in Cuba.

GLOSSARY

Obá	The Yoruba word for king, and one of the words used in Lucumí to designate a master of ceremonies.
Obá-oríaté	A ceremonial master of Lucumí and a master diviner of the Dilogún.
Obatalá	The wise and truthful Orisha who created the human body and who is older than the other Orishas.
Oshún	The orisha of sensuality and abundance, who in her later years became a profound mystic. Oshún is identified with sweet water in rivers and lakes.
Odu	The codified symbols and verses which are the fundamental elements of both Dilogún and Ifá divination.
Ogún	The orisha of metal, of blacksmiths, and of the knife. It is in his name that a priest sacrifices an animal.
Oracle	The word oracle comes from the Latin word meaning to pray; it is also connected to the word for mouth. In this sense, the diviner, or oracle, is the mouth of spirit.
Oríaté	One who divines on a mat and interprets the Dilogún.
Orisha	The pantheon of Yoruba gods, or an individual member of that pantheon. The Yoruba say there are 401 orisha, divine beings with superhuman powers, but only a few are recognized in the Diaspora. The word is both singular and plural.
Orúnmìlà	He is the god of the Ifá divination. Orúnmìlà learned Ifá from an ancient Iroko tree.
Oyá	She is identified with the whirlwind and thunder. Oyá transports the spirits of deceased people to peace in the afterlife.
Padrino	The Spanish word for godfather, referring to the male who initiates a person into Lucumí and who guides that person's development in the religion.
Shangó	The orisha of thunder, justice, resurrection. He was also a general and king of the Oyo Empire.

BIBLIOGRAPHY

Bresson, David, *Scientific American*, February 19, 2012, online.

Dennis, Andy, *Mountains—People and Mountains*, in *Te Ara, the Encyclopaedia of New Zealand*, online.

Eng, Sheri, *Trees Pay Us Back—Urban Trees Make a Good Investment*, Pacific Southwest Research Station/USDA Forest Service News Release, 2011.

Eisley, Loren, *The Firmament of Time*, Bison Books, 1999.

Graham-McLay, Charlotte, *Māori Language Having a Renaissance in New Zealand*, www.nytimes.com/20/18/09/16/world,asia/new-zealand, 2018.

Harris, Judith, *Jung and Yoga: The Psyche Body Connection*, Inner City Books, 2001.

Huang, Alford trans., *The Complete I Ching*, Inner Traditions, Vermont.

Kimmerer, Robin, *Braiding Sweet Grass*, Milkweed Editions, 2013.

Lyver et al., *Tūhoe Tuawhenua Mātauranga of Kererū 7, New Zealand Journal of Ecology* (2008) 32 (1): 7-17 ©New Zealand Ecological Society. Available on-line at: http://www.newzealandecology.org/nzje/Tūhoe Tuawhenua mātauranga of kererū (Hemiphaga novaseelandiae novaseelandiae).

Mitchell, Hilary and John, *Te Tau Ihu O Te Waka*, Vol IV, Ngāti Tama ki Te Waipounamu o Te Waka-a-Maui Trust, 2014.

O'Connor, Bessie, *The Māori in the Landscape*, booklet, unpublished.

Robertson, Maurice, *Wainui Bay*, Takaka Library, reference copy, self-published, 1972.

Simpson, Philip, *Down the Bay: A Natural and Cultural History of Abel Tasman National Park*, Potton and Burton, Nelson, 2018.

ACKNOWLEDGEMENTS

First, I want to thank those who are my team. Ernesto Pichardo has been my teacher of Lucumi for over thirty years. More than a body of ritual and stories, Ernesto has taught me the nature of *spirit*. We have spent scores of hours discussing spiritual aspects of life together, in Miami where Ernesto lives and where I lived for many years. Aroha Ropata is the Māori woman who inspired me with her knowledge of the Waitaha people, and her decades long friendship which I treasure. Keith Hill, Auckland publisher of Attar Books, suggested this book to me and edited it with such clarity he can only have made *Prophecy* a better book. Dr. Richard Schwartz, Emeritus Professor of English, helped me by editing an earlier book, *The Soothsayer*, until it was readable and tight; *Prophecy on the River* contains themes from *The Soothsayer*.

Prophecy is a memoir. It is my recollection of life here on my land in Wainui Bay and my reflections on the landscape around me. I have used methods that are anthropological, research with books and publications, and methods that are intuitive and have evolved as I developed my skills as a diviner over several decades. Divination is an ancient way of talking and consulting with wise and sage spirits. It has a strong moral core.

I am anthropologist and an artist, and have done research with Yoruba people in West Africa, who are ancestors of the Lucumi religion in Miami and Cuba. I have worked with Ernesto, a well-known leader of Lucumi in the United States and Cuba, for over thirty years. He is my Padrino, my teacher, and I owe him a large debt of gratitude. I thank him again for his prescient divinations and mediumship which form the basis of *Prophecy*'s title.

I apologise to the Māori in advance because I know I can't have gotten everything right. I am a true beginner in Māori history, culture and language. My interpretations of the deeply moving Māori philosophy of nature are my own, but are inspired by Māori stories and proverbs.

My wonderful husband, John McKie, has been with me through all the events in the book. His courage and strength, tireless work and organisational skills, have made Waitaha possible.

And to those local friends who read a few chapters of this book or critiqued the cover, your energy deeply appreciated: Anita Peters, Murray Hedwig, Grant Knowles, Tracey Smith, Lethea Erz and Elisabeth Von Madarasz. To Elisabeth I owe special thanks for pointing out my ambiguous use of "Waitaha" in an earlier draft.

And to all the Māori people who were so generous on my recent North Island trip, and who helped me understand the spirit of the Māori people. I say a special thanks to Josie Henihau, the curator of Māori artifacts in Opotiki, and to Brad whose ancestors in the Waikato were buried in a mass grave. Finally, a big thanks to Wainui's local mana whenua, who although few in number contribute a large amount to our small community. I have especially learned from them in the ceremonies outside for a park or a newly introduced bird. They make the profane, sacred.

www.ingramcontent.com/pod-product-compliance
Lightning Source LLC
Chambersburg PA
CBHW020258030426
42336CB00010B/829